The WATERMARK
Restaurant COOKBOOK

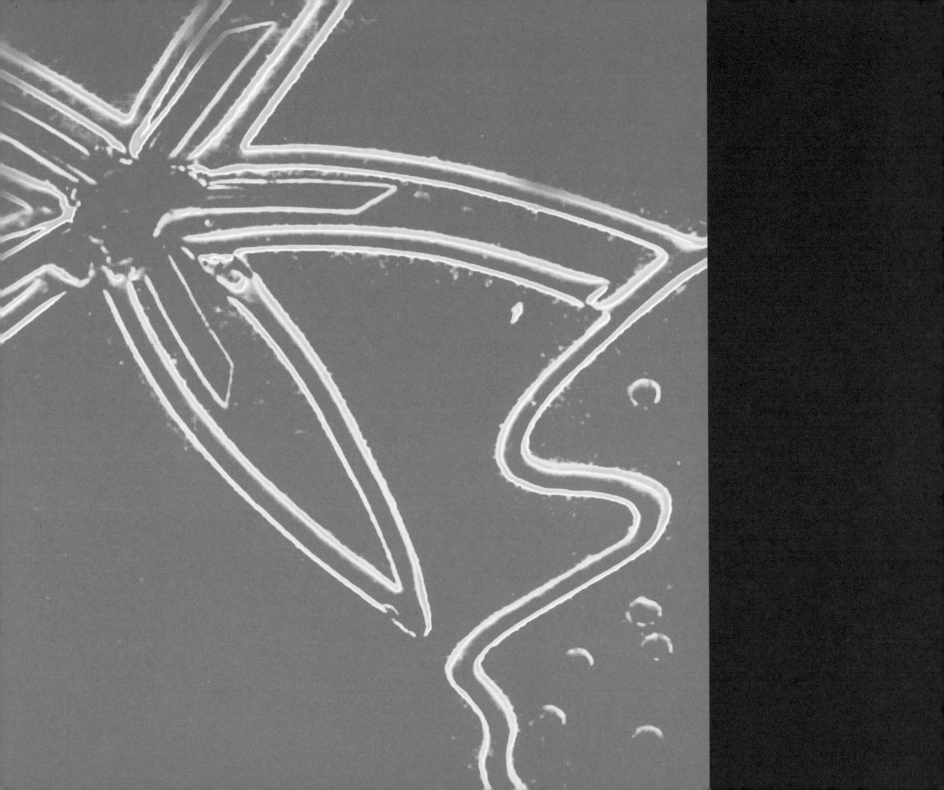

fusion

KENNETH LEUNG

MARK WILSON *and* CAROLE RUTA

PHOTOGRAPHY *by* WARWICK KENT

Angus&Robertson

An imprint of HarperCollins*Publishers*

Angus&Robertson
An imprint of HarperCollins*Publishers*

First published in Australia in 1997
Copyright © Kenneth Leung, Carole Ruta and Mark Wilson, 1997

HarperCollins*Publishers*
25 Ryde Road, Pymble, Sydney NSW 2073, Australia
31 View Road, Glenfield, Auckland 10, New Zealand
77–85 Fulham Palace Road, London W6 8JB, United Kingdom
Hazelton Lanes, 55 Avenue Road, Suite 2900, Toronto, Ontario M5R 3L2
and 1995 Markham Road, Scarborough, Ontario M1B 5M8, Canada
10 East 53rd Street, New York NY 10032, USA

National Library of Australia Cataloguing-in-Publication data:

Leung, Kenneth H. K. (Kenneth Hing Kwan).
    Fusion : the Watermark Restaurant cookbook.

    Includes index.
    ISBN 0 207 19182 4.

    1. Watermark Restaurant. 2. Cookery. 3. Restaurants – New South Wales –
    Sydney. I. Ruta, Carole. II. Wilson, Mark L. (Mark Lang). III. Title.

641.5

Photography by Warwick Kent.

Produced by Phoenix Offset in Hong Kong on 140 gsm Woodfree.

WATER*M*MARK

FOREWORD

Kenneth and I had a dream ~
to create a world-class restaurant on Sydney Harbour.
From the outset, we pictured exactly how the restaurant would look and operate, right down to the finest detail.
That vision is as strong as ever, and it is the base from which we continually
strive for excellence and success.

Great food, great service and great value are the key philosophies at Watermark. We believe our cuisine to be unique. With his classical techniques, Asian heritage and creative genius, Kenneth produces food that allows the flavours to dance over your tastebuds. We believe in stylish and intuitive service, which is why our staff are put through rigorous training. We uphold value by ensuring that our food and service are consistently world-class. As one of Sydney's

finer dining venues, our promise is 'to deliver everything on time, every time, exactly as promised'.

Kenneth and I thank you for the opportunity of bringing a piece of Watermark Restaurant into your home. I hope that our Watermark recipes inspire you to unleash your creative cooking potential. Enjoy.

Mark Wilson

INTRODUCTION

I first met Kenneth Leung and Mark Wilson in 1990. What singularly impressed me with Ken's menu was his total confidence in disregarding the conventional. His blend of flavours was adventurous and exciting, giving my palate some of the most wonderful taste sensations I had ever experienced.

When I put to Kenneth and Mark the idea of producing a Watermark cookbook, Kenneth had reservations. He had nothing formally written down – his recipes were mostly in his head with perhaps a few scribbled notes in Cantonese. What's more, preparing restaurant food is a far cry from cooking in the home kitchen for four people. But with the help of my agent, Fitzroy Boulting, the Watermark team was won over.

Countless hours were then spent at The Watermark discussing ingredients, cooking techniques and especially preparation methods – the restaurant staff were unfailing in their support during this book's development, and I thank them for that. Although I speak no Cantonese and English is not Kenneth's first language, Kenneth's patience and wonderful sense of humour enabled me to gain a deep insight into the passion and philosophy behind his food.

Commercial kitchen equipment, especially stoves and grillers, vary dramatically in temperature ranges to the domestic variety so Watermark cuisine took over my home while all the recipes, amounts and timings were thoroughly tested.

All recipes in the *Fusion* cookbook are for four people, unless otherwise stated, making it easy to increase for six or eight people or to halve the quantities for two.

The theme of Watermark is fusion – many nations' ingredients and approaches to cuisine are amalgamated with traditional techniques. The results are exciting, as you will also discover.

My knowledge has been greatly enriched by working with Kenneth Leung and I hope you enjoy exploring these recipes as much as I enjoyed writing them.

Carole Ruta

Matching Food with Wine

Tradition dictates that dry sherry is served with consommé; delicate white wines with fish; fuller-bodied white wines with white meats; light red wines with game meats; red wines with red meats; sauternes with dessert; and port with cheese. Champagne is served at celebrations.

This formula falls short with food that crosses conventional boundaries, for it fails to take into account how a dish is prepared. Is it steamed, baked or fried? What other ingredients are in the dish, and indeed what components are in the accompanying sauces?

Wines defy stereotypes. A cool-climate Tasmanian chardonnay will lean towards citrus/grapefruit characteristics while a chardonnay from the warmer region of the Barossa Valley will show more peach, melon and fig characters. Similarly, shiraz shows pepper and spice overtones from a cooler climate producer and ripe plum flavours from a hotter region.

Body – a wine's texture and weight – plays the key role when trying to create a perfect partnership between food and wine. Delicate food styles need delicate, lighter-bodied wines; heavier dishes can cope with more robust, fuller-bodied wines. Colour is not the determiner. It is now widely accepted that some red wines can happily harmonise with fish; in fact a pinot noir is a perfect partner for tuna or Atlantic salmon.

The flavour components of a dish need to complement the flavour components of the wine. Wine will taste acidic if served with very sweet food, unless the wine is sweeter than the food. In comparison, food with a high acid content can flatter a slightly acidic wine.

Matching Food with Wine

There can be no right or wrong on the level of personal enjoyment when it comes to wine and food matching. We all have different palates, rather like fingerprints, and it is only with experimentation and trust in restaurant sommeliers that wine and food marriages can be made in heaven. These are simply general and logical criteria that can be applied to enhance the enjoyment of the wining and dining experience. The main objective is to enjoy.

Wines for fusion food

That fact that wines vary from region to region and vintage to vintage makes it difficult to apply strict rules about wine and food matching. The Watermark staff are trained to advise customers on wine selection, and the restaurant's wine list covers the diverse wine regions of Australia and New Zealand, embracing boutique vineyards and large wineries. It reflects the style of food which Kenneth Leung creates, but the list also changes with the seasons.

Sauvignon blanc, semillon/sauvignon blanc, gewürztraminer, riesling, verdelho, colombard and unwooded chardonnays play a major role through the summer months. Oaked chardonnays come out of hibernation in the colder months to partner the more robust food styles of autumn and winter. Chambourcin, merlot and pinot complement the spice elements of Kenneth's menu throughout the lazy days of summer, and luscious full-bodied shiraz plays its part in the food and wine partnership during the windswept, chilly days when comfort flavours are in demand.

PRAWN WONTONS

125 GRAMS RAW PRAWN MEAT,
  CHOPPED SMALL

2 TABLESPOONS BAMBOO SHOOTS,
  FINELY CHOPPED

¼ TEASPOON SUGAR

3 DROPS SESAME OIL

1 TEASPOON CORNFLOUR

1 EGG WHITE, LIGHTLY BEATEN

SALT AND PEPPER

20 WONTON PASTRY WRAPPERS

2 CUPS VEGETABLE OIL

Mix the prawn meat, bamboo shoots, sugar and sesame oil.

Sprinkle with the cornflour, add the egg white and mix thoroughly.

Season to taste.

Divide the mixture between the wonton pastry wrappers. Moisten the edges of the wrappers with a little water.

Lift the four sides and pinch them together to encase the filling.

Heat the oil in a wok and stir-fry the wontons until they are golden brown; drain on paper towels and serve immediately.

Note: The wontons may also be steamed in an oiled steamer-basket for 5 minutes.

HERB *and* GARLIC CHEESE WONTONS

125 GRAMS CREAM CHEESE

1 CLOVE GARLIC, FINELY CHOPPED

2 TABLESPOONS TARRAGON LEAVES,
  CHOPPED

SALT AND PEPPER

20 WONTON PASTRY WRAPPERS

2 CUPS VEGETABLE OIL

Mix the cream cheese, garlic and tarragon.

Season to taste.

Divide the mixture between the wonton pastry wrappers.

Moisten the edges of the pastry with a little water.

Lift the four sides and pinch them together to encase the filling.

Heat the oil in a wok and stir-fry the wontons until they are golden brown; drain on paper towels and serve immediately.

Accompany with Cherry Tomato Compote (see page 168) or Riesling Sauce (see page 42).

HERB *and* GARLIC CHEESE WONTONS

ATLANTIC SALMON WONTONS

125 GRAMS RAW ATLANTIC SALMON,
    FINELY DICED
1 TEASPOON WHITE ONION, MINCED
1 TEASPOON LEMON JUICE
1 TEASPOON CHERVIL, CHOPPED
1 EGG WHITE, LIGHTLY BEATEN
2 DROPS TABASCO SAUCE
SALT AND PEPPER
20 WONTON PASTRY WRAPPERS
OIL FOR DEEP FRYING

Place the salmon, onion, lemon juice, chervil, egg white and Tabasco sauce in a food processor or blender; pulse to combine.

Season to taste.

Divide the mixture between the wonton wrappers.

Moisten the edges of the pastry with a little water.

Lift the four sides and pinch them together to encase the filling.

Heat the oil in a wok and stir-fry the wontons until they are golden brown. Drain on paper towels and serve immediately.

Include as part of an Asian antipasto selection.

STEAMED VARIATION

Brush a steamer-basket with oil (to avoid sticking) and place over boiling water.

Sit the wontons in the basket and steam for 5 minutes.

VARIATION

To make this mixture into ravioli or cappelletti, follow the recipe but increase the number of wonton wrappers to 40.

Divide the mixture between 20 wonton wrappers, moisten the edges and lay another wonton wrapper on top, pressing down the edges to seal.

Poach in simmering stock or water for approximately 5 minutes or until the pastry is cooked.

Remove with a slotted spoon.

Serve with Ginger and White Wine Sauce or Light Curry Sauce (see page 157).

MIXED MUSHROOM GOW GEE

50 GRAMS DRIED WHITE FUNGI

50 GRAMS DRIED BLACK FUNGI

50 GRAMS DRIED SHIITAKE MUSHROOMS

50 GRAMS DRIED VEGETABLES

HOT WATER

50 GRAMS OYSTER MUSHROOMS,
   FINELY SLICED

50 GRAMS BUTTON MUSHROOMS,
   FINELY SLICED

1 TABLESPOON VEGETABLE OIL

1 TABLESPOON SPRING ONIONS, FINELY
   CHOPPED

2 CM PIECE OF FRESH GINGER,
   PEELED, LIGHTLY CRUSHED AND KEPT
   IN THE PIECE

2 TABLESPOONS CORIANDER LEAVES,
   CHOPPED

½ CUP OYSTER SAUCE

2 TABLESPOONS WHITE SUGAR

500 ML WATER

1 TABLESPOON CORNFLOUR

2 TABLESPOONS WATER

1 TABLESPOON VEGETABLE OIL

1 PACKET GOW GEE PASTRY (OR SEE PAGE 17)

Soak the dried white and black fungi, shiitake mushrooms and dried vegetables in hot water for 2 hours to soften.

Drain and squeeze dry, remove and discard any stems, and chop into small pieces. Mix with the sliced oyster and button mushrooms.

Heat the oil in a frypan, add the spring onions and ginger, then sauté for 1 minute.

Add the mushroom mixture and coriander leaves, then sauté for a further 2 minutes.

Add the oyster sauce and stir.

Add the sugar and 500 ml water.

Reduce, stirring occasionally, until the mushrooms are soft and the liquid is almost evaporated. Remove the ginger and discard.

Combine the cornflour with 1 tablespoon of the water and mix to a smooth paste.

Remove the mushroom mixture from the heat and stir through the cornflour paste.

Stir in 1 tablespoon of vegetable oil.

Allow to cool completely (the oil stops the mixture from becoming dry when cooked).

Place a heaped teaspoon of the mushroom mixture in the centre of each gow gee pastry.

Moisten the edges of the pastry with a little water. Pinch the edges together tightly, making pleats, to encase the mixture.

Steam the gow gee in an oiled steamer-basket for 5 minutes or wok-fry until golden brown, then drain on paper towels.

VARIATION

For a different texture heat a little oil in a frypan, then fry the gow gee, flat side down, to crisp the bottom.

Add half a cup of water, cover and cook until the water has evaporated (6–8 minutes).

The gow gee will then be crispy on the bottom and soft on the top.

GOW GEE VARIATIONS

Sweet Potato and Corn Gow Gee

1 TABLESPOON ONION, MINCED

½ TEASPOON VEGETABLE OIL

250 GRAMS SWEET POTATO, COOKED
  AND MASHED

100 GRAMS SWEET CORN KERNELS, COOKED

½ TEASPOON NUTMEG

1 PACKET GOW GEE PASTRY (OR SEE PAGE 17)

Spinach Gow Gee

1 BUNCH ENGLISH SPINACH LEAVES,
  WASHED WELL

½ TABLESPOON VEGETABLE OIL

1 TABLESPOON ONION, FINELY CHOPPED

1 CLOVE GARLIC, FINELY CHOPPED

½ TEASPOON NUTMEG

1 TABLESPOON CORNFLOUR

2 TABLESPOONS WATER

1 PACKET GOW GEE PASTRY (OR SEE PAGE 17)

SWEET POTATO AND CORN GOW GEE

Sauté the onion in hot vegetable oil until it is soft.

Add the mashed sweet potato, cooked corn kernels and nutmeg. Mix thoroughly.

Proceed as per recipe for Mixed Mushroom Gow Gee (see page 15)

Note: Makes approximately 40.

SPINACH GOW GEE

Quickly blanch the spinach in boiling water.

Drain and immediately refresh in icy cold water. Drain again, squeeze dry, then chop finely.

Heat the oil and sauté the onion and garlic until they are soft.

Add the spinach and nutmeg, then sauté for 1 minute.

Dissolve the cornflour in the water and add to the spinach mixture.

Remove from the heat, stirring to combine. Allow to cool.

Proceed as per recipe for Mixed Mushroom Gow Gee (see page 15).

Note: Makes approximately 40.

WONTON PASTRY

300 GRAMS SOFT FLOUR
  (AVAILABLE AT ITALIAN DELICATESSENS)
2 EGGS, LIGHTLY BEATEN
2 EGG WHITES, LIGHTLY BEATEN
1 TEASPOON VEGETABLE OIL
PINCH OF SALT

Place all the ingredients in a food processor or blender and process until they are just combined. Take care not to over-process.

Remove the mixture to a lightly floured board and knead it until it is smooth and elastic. Add a little more flour if the dough is too wet or a few drops of water if the dough is too dry.

Roll the dough into a ball and cover with plastic wrap.

Refrigerate for 1 hour.

Using a pasta machine, roll out the dough as thinly as possible and cut it into 8 cm squares.

Note: This is really for the purist. Pre-made wonton wrappers are readily available at Asian grocery shops and many supermarkets.

GOW GEE PASTRY

3 CUPS SOFT FLOUR
  (AVAILABLE AT ITALIAN DELICATESSENS)
1 CUP WATER
1 TABLESPOON VEGETABLE OIL
PINCH OF SALT

Mix all the ingredients and knead well.

Using a pasta machine, roll out the dough as thinly as possible and cut it into 7 cm rounds.

Note: Gow Gee pastry is readily available at Asian grocery shops and many supermarkets and is perfect for the home cook to use.

PAPERBARK OYSTERS

1 TEASPOON VEGETABLE OIL

5 JUNIPER BERRIES, CRUSHED

1 TABLESPOON SUGAR

1 TEASPOON DRIED MIXED HERBS

10 CM SQUARE OF PAPERBARK,
 CUT UP OR TORN INTO PIECES

12 FRESH OYSTERS, OPENED,
 ON THE SHELL

1 TABLESPOON WATER

LEMON WEDGES

Place the oil, juniper berries, sugar, mixed herbs and paperbark in a heavy-based frypan.

Evenly distribute the oysters (in their shells) on top.

Cover the pan and place it over high heat until the pan starts to smoke (2–3 minutes).

Remove the lid and add the water to the pan, avoiding the oysters.

Cover and return to the heat, allow to smoke for another minute.

Remove from the heat and serve immediately with lemon wedges.

Note: The paperbark from this recipe can be used more than once. Discard when it has burnt through.

GINGER *and* SOY STEAMED OYSTERS

12 FRESH OYSTERS, OPENED,
 ON THE SHELL

2 CM PIECE GINGER, PEELED AND CUT
 INTO FINE JULIENNE THREADS

1 TABLESPOON CORIANDER LEAVES,
 FINELY CHOPPED

12 TEASPOONS LIGHT SOY SAUCE

12 TEASPOONS VEGETABLE OIL

Place the oysters (in their shells) on a plate or tray that will fit into a steamer-basket.

Put 3–4 threads of ginger on each oyster, then sprinkle with chopped coriander.

Add 1 teaspoon of light soy sauce to each oyster.

Place the plate or tray in a steamer-basket over hot water. Cover and steam for 2 minutes.

Heat the oil to smoking hot in a small pan and pour 1 teaspoon over each oyster.

Serve immediately.

Notes: It's critical to get the temperature of the oil right so that it amalgamates the flavours without giving an 'oily' taste.

If any juices escape onto the plate, spoon them over the oysters before serving.

PAPERBARK OYSTERS *and* GINGER *and* SOY STEAMED OYSTERS

STEAMED CRAB NORI ROLL

200 GRAMS FRESH CRABMEAT, COOKED

200 GRAMS BONELESS WHITE FISH (BLUE-EYE COD OR SIMILAR), DICED

2 TABLESPOONS ONION, FINELY CHOPPED OR GRATED

1 TABLESPOON WHITE WINE

1 TEASPOON LEMON JUICE

1 TEASPOON BRANDY

1 TEASPOON PERNOD

2 TABLESPOONS FLAT-LEAF PARSLEY LEAVES, FINELY CHOPPED

½ TEASPOON PAPRIKA

2 DROPS TABASCO SAUCE

1 EGG WHITE

SALT AND PEPPER TO TASTE

2 SHEETS NORI (ROASTED SEAWEED)

Place the crabmeat, fish, onion, white wine, lemon juice, brandy, Pernod, parsley, paprika and Tabasco sauce in a food processor or blender and pulse quickly to combine.

Add the egg white and seasoning.

Pulse for a few seconds until just combined.

Spread the mixture over two sheets of nori.

Roll up firmly.

With a sharp knife, carefully cut the nori roll into 3 cm lengths.

Place in an oiled steamer-basket and steam over hot water for 5 minutes.

Serve immediately as part of an antipasto platter.

Notes: The filling is easier to combine quickly if all the ingredients are cold.

This makes an elegant entrée, served with beurre blanc or light hollandaise sauce.

CRAB CAKES VARIATION

To turn the above mixture into crab cakes, simply add a large potato, peeled, grated and washed to remove excess starch, and 1 tablespoon of chopped coriander to the mixture.

Blend well.

Shape into bite-sized cakes. Pan-fry in a little oil for approximately 2 minutes each side.

Serve immediately.

Steamed Crab Nori Roll

STUFFED CHINESE MUSHROOMS

Mushrooms

16 CHINESE DRIED MUSHROOMS,
  ABOUT THE SAME SIZE
HOT WATER
1 TABLESPOON VEGETABLE OIL
2 CM PIECE GINGER, SLICED
3 SHALLOTS, CHOPPED FINELY
½ CUP OYSTER SAUCE
1 TABLESPOON SUGAR
500 ML WATER

Filling

150 GRAMS RAW PRAWN MEAT,
  FINELY CHOPPED
1 TABLESPOON CORIANDER LEAVES,
  CHOPPED
1 SMALL RED CHILLI, SEEDED AND
  FINELY CHOPPED
1 TEASPOON LEMON GRASS,
  FINELY CHOPPED
1 TABLESPOON WHITE WINE
1 TABLESPOON BRANDY
1 TEASPOON SESAME OIL
1 EGG WHITE, LIGHTLY BEATEN
SALT AND PEPPER

MUSHROOMS

Soak the dried mushrooms in the hot water for 2 hours to soften.

Drain, remove and discard any stems.

Squeeze out any excess moisture.

Sauté the ginger and shallots in the oil until they are soft.

Add the mushrooms and sauté for another minute.

Add the oyster sauce, sugar and water; simmer for 30 minutes or until the mushrooms are soft and most of the moisture has evaporated.

Allow to cool completely.

FILLING

Mix all the ingredients, adding the egg white and seasoning last.

Spoon into the cold mushroom caps; steam in an oiled steamer-basket for 5 minutes.

VARIATIONS

Substitute minced raw pork or chicken for the prawn meat and use fresh tarragon leaves or chervil instead of the coriander.

This mixture can also be used to stuff capsicum pieces.

Pan-fry the capsicum pieces, stuffing side down, for 2 minutes.

Turn and cook with the capsicum side down for a further 3 minutes.

STUFFED CHINESE MUSHROOMS

CURRIED POTATO *and* GREEN BEAN PARCELS

2 TABLESPOONS VEGETABLE OIL

1 TABLESPOON ONION, FINELY CHOPPED

200 GRAMS POTATOES, FINELY DICED,
THEN WASHED TO REMOVE STARCH

100 GRAMS GREEN BEANS, TOPPED AND
TAILED AND FINELY SLICED

2 TEASPOONS CURRY POWDER

2 TABLESPOONS WATER

SALT AND PEPPER TO TASTE

8 SPRING-ROLL WRAPPERS

2 CUPS VEGETABLE OIL

Heat the oil in a frypan and sauté the onion until it is soft.

Add the potatoes; toss well to coat with oil.

Add the green beans and cook, stirring constantly, for approximately 4 minutes.

Add the curry powder; stir to release aromas.

Add the water and cook until combined.

The mixture should be sticky rather than wet.

Season to taste and allow to cool.

Divide the cooled mixture between the spring-roll wrappers and roll up, enclosing the mixture.

Heat the remainder of the oil in a wok and stir-fry the parcels until they are golden.

Drain on paper towels and serve immediately.

SHANGHAI NOODLES

500 GRAMS SHANGHAI NOODLES
(AVAILABLE AT ASIAN GROCERY SHOPS)

3 TABLESPOONS BUTTER

4 TABLESPOONS FRENCH ESCHALOTS,
FINELY CHOPPED

60 ML VODKA (2 NIPS)

4–6 TABLESPOONS CAVIAR OR
TASMANIAN SALMON ROE

4 TABLESPOONS CHIVES, FINELY CHOPPED

SALT AND PEPPER TO TASTE

EXTRA CAVIAR AND CHIVES FOR GARNISH

Cook the noodles as per the manufacturer's instructions; drain and keep warm.

Melt the butter in a large frypan and add the eschalots; sauté until they are soft.

Add the vodka and stir until all the alcohol is released.

Turn down the heat and add the caviar; sauté for a few seconds to combine.

Add the noodles and toss to heat through.

Add the chives and seasoning and stir quickly to combine.

Remove the pan from the heat.

Serve immediately, dividing the noodles between four warm plates.

Garnish with the extra caviar and chives.

Notes: This recipe was given to Kenneth 10 years ago by the Head Chef of The Mandarin Hotel, Hong Kong.

If you don't have any vodka on hand, substitute dry vermouth.

SHANGHAI NOODLES

CHIU CHOW SQUID-INK NOODLES

375 GRAMS SQUID-INK PASTA (AVAILABLE
AT SPECIALTY GROCERY SHOPS)

3 TABLESPOONS BUTTER

6 SHALLOTS, FINELY CHOPPED

90 ML (3 NIPS) DRY VERMOUTH OR
DRY SHERRY

2–3 TABLESPOONS CHIU CHOW CHILLI OIL
(AVAILABLE AT ASIAN GROCERY SHOPS)

SALT TO TASTE

Cook the squid-ink pasta until *al dente*.

Drain and keep warm.

Melt the butter in a large frypan and sauté
the shallots.

Add the vermouth or sherry and stir over
high heat to release the alcohol.

Turn down the heat to medium and add
the Chiu Chow chilli oil.

Stir and add the pasta, tossing to
warm through.

Season with salt and serve immediately on
four warm plates.

*Notes: Chiu Chow chilli oil is imported
from China and made from preserved chillies
and fermented soya beans – there is no suitable
substitute for this sauce.*

*The amount of chilli oil is critical – using less oil
results in a bland flavour.*

This hot and spicy dish is a must for chilli lovers.

VARIATION

For a more substantial dish, serve topped
with sautéed scallops or grilled prawns.

CHIU CHOW SQUID-INK NOODLES

OVEN-DRIED VEGETABLES *and* NOODLE SALAD

1 LARGE ZUCCHINI, CUT INTO BATONS

1 LARGE RED CAPSICUM, CUT INTO
  BATONS

4 ROMA TOMATOES, CUT LENGTHWISE
  INTO 6

½ LARGE EGGPLANT, SKIN OFF

1 TEASPOON TABASCO SAUCE

1 TEASPOON SWEET PAPRIKA

1 TEASPOON SUGAR

1 TEASPOON COARSE GROUND
  BLACK PEPPER

¼ CUP OLIVE OIL

1 TABLESPOON LEMON JUICE

1 TABLESPOON BASIL LEAVES,
  ROUGHLY CHOPPED

SALT TO TASTE

300 GRAMS JAPANESE BUCKWHEAT
  NOODLES

Preheat the oven to 220°C.

Combine the zucchini, capsicum, tomatoes, eggplant, Tabasco sauce, sweet paprika, sugar, black pepper and olive oil.

Toss to coat with the oil.

Arrange on a flat oven tray in one layer and place in the preheated oven.

Reduce the heat to 150°C and cook for 20–30 minutes.

The vegetables should be firm but cooked.

Remove from the oven and allow to cool.

Add the lemon juice and chopped basil.

Season with salt.

Cook the noodles in plenty of boiling water, according to the manufacturer's instructions, until they are *al dente*.

Drain, refresh in cold water and drain again.

To serve, warm four plates, make a 'nest' of noodles on each one and top with the cooled roasted vegetables.

Oven-Dried Vegetables *and* Noodle Salad

STIR-FRIED BEEF *and* NOODLES

2 TABLESPOONS LIGHT SOY SAUCE

1 TABLESPOON VEGETABLE OIL

1 TEASPOON SUGAR

1 TABLESPOON CORNFLOUR

3–4 DROPS TABASCO SAUCE

1 CUP COLD WATER

½ TEASPOON BICARBONATE OF SODA

600 GRAMS BEEF FILLET, CUT INTO STRIPS

400 GRAMS SPAGHETTI OR LINGUINE
  NOODLES

1 CUP VEGETABLE OIL

1 TABLESPOON VEGETABLE OIL

4 FRENCH ESCHALOTS, FINELY CHOPPED

1 TABLESPOON GARLIC, FINELY CHOPPED

1 TABLESPOON LEMONGRASS, FINELY
  CHOPPED

2 TABLESPOONS FISH SAUCE

200 GRAMS FRESH BEAN SHOOTS,
  WASHED AND DRAINED

2 TABLESPOONS CORIANDER LEAVES,
  CHOPPED

Combine the soy sauce, vegetable oil, sugar, cornflour, Tabasco sauce, water and bicarbonate of soda; add the beef strips and leave to marinate for at least 30 minutes.

Cook the spaghetti or linguine in plenty of boiling water, according to the manufacturer's instructions, until *al dente*.

Drain, refresh in a little cold water, drain again and put aside.

Heat 1 cup of oil in a wok until smoking.

Add the beef strips and stir vigorously for 1 minute.

Remove the beef with a slotted spoon and drain off any excess oil.

In a clean wok, heat 1 tablespoon of oil and stir-fry the eschalots, garlic and lemongrass for 2 minutes.

Add the noodles and stir to heat through. Add the fish sauce and bean shoots; toss quickly to combine. Add the coriander, toss and serve immediately.

Note: When Kenneth and I first discussed this recipe I was shocked at the amount of water in the marinade and also the oil for cooking.

Frankly, I doubted it would work. But I followed the recipe to the letter and I was amazed at how the marinade 'disappeared' into the meat.

After frying, the texture of the meat was like sheer silk and melted away in the mouth with no hint of a greasy after-taste.

VARIATIONS

This is a basic recipe that can be built on.

Replace the bean shoots with a bunch of fresh asparagus, chopped and blanched.

Add 2 tablespoons of black bean sauce and some sautéed mushrooms. Substitute chicken breasts for the beef.

The alternatives are endless, use your imagination and have fun.

NOODLES *and* EGG PASTRY

PRAWN RAVIOLI *in* SEAFOOD BROTH

Ravioli

150 GRAMS GREEN PRAWN MEAT, MINCED

½ ONION, MINCED

1 TABLESPOON WHITE WINE

SALT AND PEPPER TO TASTE

12 SHEETS EGG PASTRY (AVAILABLE AT
  ASIAN GROCERY SHOPS)

12 WHOLE GREEN PRAWNS

Seafood Broth

1 LITRE SEAFOOD STOCK (SEE PAGE 153)

½ CUP MILK

½ CUP WHITE WINE

1 SPRIG FRESH THYME

1 BAYLEAF

SALT AND PEPPER TO TASTE

Garnish

1 CARROT, PEELED AND CUT INTO BATONS

1 CELERY STICK, WASHED AND CUT INTO
  BATONS

1 BUNCH BOK CHOY LEAVES, WASHED

100 GRAMS BABY ENGLISH SPINACH
  LEAVES, WASHED WELL

RAVIOLI

Combine the prawn meat, onion, white wine
and seasoning.

Divide the mixture onto the egg pastry sheets
and top each one with a green prawn.

Fold the pastry over into a triangle, encasing
the filling, and turn the points inwards to
make a dumpling.

Poach the dumplings in simmering water
for 2 minutes, then turn them over and poach
for a further 2 minutes.

If you are using a small saucepan, poach the
dumplings in two batches for even cooking.

SEAFOOD BROTH

Heat all the ingredients until simmering and
reduce to approximately 1 litre.

GARNISH

Simmer the carrot and celery batons in
the hot broth for 3 minutes.

Add the bok choy leaves, then simmer
the mixture for 1 minute.

Add the spinach leaves, then remove
the broth from the heat.

TO ASSEMBLE

With a slotted spoon, divide the vegetables
between four warm soup plates.

Top each plate with three warm prawn ravioli
and pour over the hot stock.

Serve immediately.

PRAWN RAVIOLI *in* SEAFOOD BROTH

STICKY RICE *in a* BANANA LEAF

2 CUPS SHORT GRAIN GLUTINOUS RICE
  (AVAILABLE AT ASIAN GROCERY SHOPS)

2 LITRES WARM WATER

2 TABLESPOONS OLIVE OIL

1 TEASPOON OLIVE OIL

1 ONION, FINELY DICED

1 STICK CELERY, FINELY DICED

1 X 2 CM PIECE FRESH GINGER, PEELED

100 GRAMS MUSHROOM GOW GEE
  MIXTURE (SEE PAGE 15)

¼ CUP CHICKEN STOCK (SEE PAGE 152)

2 TABLESPOONS OYSTER SAUCE

GROUND WHITE PEPPER TO TASTE

4 BANANA LEAVES, WASHED AND LIGHTLY
  OILED ON BOTH SIDES

Place the rice in the warm water, cover and leave for 2 hours.

Strain, add the oil and mix through.

Spread the rice, 3–4 cm thick, into a cake tin; place it in a steamer basket over hot water.

Cover and steam for 20 minutes.

Heat 1 teaspoon of olive oil in a pan and sauté the onion, celery and ginger until the onion is soft.

Add the mushroom gow gee mixture, then sauté for 2 minutes.

Remove the ginger and add the rice, separating the grains.

Add the stock and the oyster sauce.

Season with white pepper.

Divide the mixture between the banana leaves.

Wrap tightly, enclosing all the filling, and secure with toothpicks.

Roast in a hot oven at 200°C for 10 minutes.

Remove the toothpicks and use scissors to cut a large cross through the top of each parcel.

Serve immediately.

Note: This is a perfect casual lunch or supper dish and marries especially well with barbecued or grilled fish and meats.

STICKY RICE *in a* BANANA LEAF

VEGETABLE RISOTTO *in a* LILY LEAF

4 CUPS CHICKEN STOCK (SEE PAGE 152)

4 TABLESPOONS BUTTER

1½ CUPS ARBORIO RICE

1 LARGE ZUCCHINI, CUT INTO JULIENNE STRIPS

1 RED CAPSICUM, ROASTED, PEELED, SEEDS REMOVED AND DICED

100 GRAMS DRIED SHIITAKE MUSHROOMS, SOAKED, SLICED AND COOKED AS PER RECIPE FOR STUFFED CHINESE MUSHROOMS (SEE PAGE 22)

1 CUP WHITE WINE

4 TABLESPOONS BEST QUALITY PARMESAN CHEESE, FRESHLY GRATED

4 LILY LEAVES (AVAILABLE AT ASIAN GROCERY SHOPS)

VEGETABLE OIL FOR BRUSHING

Heat the chicken stock; keep it on a simmer.

In a large saucepan melt the butter over medium heat and add the rice, stirring well to coat.

Add the zucchini, capsicum and mushrooms, then stir to combine.

Add the white wine and stir until it is almost absorbed.

Gradually add the hot chicken stock, ladle by ladle, waiting until each addition is absorbed and the rice is cooked but *al dente*.

Stir in the Parmesan.

Soak the lily leaves for 30 minutes in warm water.

Drain and dry on a clean tea towel.

Brush each side with a little oil.

Divide the risotto between the leaves and wrap up, encasing the rice, to make a neat parcel.

Secure with toothpicks.

Bake in a hot oven at 200°C for 10 minutes.

Remove the toothpicks and use scissors to cut through the top of each parcel.

Serve immediately.

VARIATION

For a vegetarian alternative, substitute vegetable stock or juice for the chicken stock.

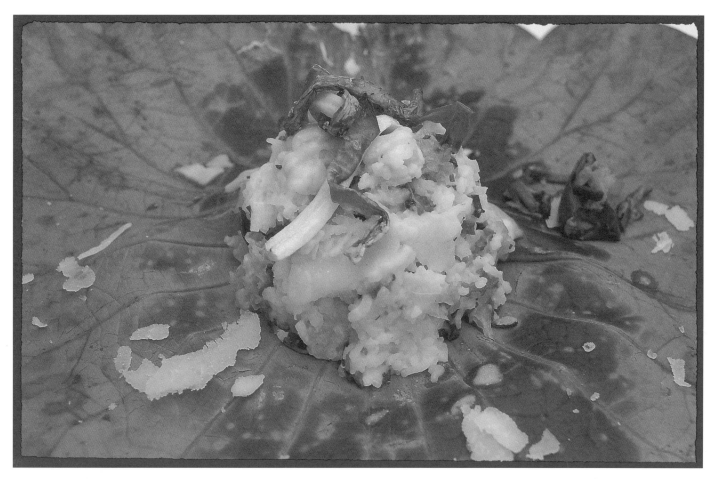

VEGETABLE RISOTTO *in a* LILY LEAF

SEAFOOD RISOTTO

Risotto

4 CUPS SEAFOOD STOCK (SEE PAGE 153)

4 TABLESPOONS OLIVE OIL

1½ CUPS ARBORIO RICE

1 CUP WHITE WINE

8 THIN SLICES PROSCIUTTO

1 CUP SEAFOOD STOCK (SEE PAGE 153)

1 TABLESPOON FLAT-LEAF PARSLEY,
  CHOPPED

Seafood

1–2 TABLESPOONS OLIVE OIL

20 PIPIS, SOAKED FOR 30 MINUTES IN COLD
  WATER TO RELEASE SAND

200 GRAMS WHITE FISH FILLETS, DEBONED
  AND CUT INTO PIECES

12 GREEN PRAWNS

12 SCALLOPS

8 BABY OCTOPUS, HEADS REMOVED

8 MORETON BAY BUG TAILS, SHELLED

200 ML SEAFOOD TOMATO SAUCE
  (SEE PAGE 160)

RISOTTO

Heat the seafood stock in a saucepan and keep it at a simmer.

Heat the oil in a large saucepan and sauté the rice to coat.

Add the white wine; stir until it is absorbed.

Slowly add the hot stock, ladle by ladle, stirring until each addition has been absorbed by the rice. Cover and leave for 5 minutes.

SEAFOOD

Heat a little oil in a wok and toss the cleaned pipis until they are just opened.

Remove to a clean bowl, reserving any juices.

On an oiled griller, char-grill each type of seafood separately until just done.

Remove and add to the pipis.

Heat the Seafood Tomato Sauce and add the seafood, toss gently to re-warm.

TO ASSEMBLE

Grill the prosciutto until it is crispy.

Heat the seafood stock until it is simmering.

Divide the risotto onto four warm plates and divide the seafood over the top.

Pour a little seafood stock on each stack of seafood.

Sprinkle with the parsley.

Lay two pieces of crisped prosciutto over each portion.

CRISPED YABBIE *and* GOAT'S CHEESE RAVIOLI
with TATSOI GREENS *and a* RIESLING SAUCE

Ravioli

100 GRAMS RAW YABBIE MEAT
  (FRESH CRAB, LOBSTER OR BUG MEAT
  CAN BE SUBSTITUTED)

1 EGG WHITE

SALT AND PEPPER TO TASTE

24 WONTON WRAPPERS (AVAILABLE IN
  ASIAN GROCERY SHOPS)

50 GRAMS FRESH SOFT GOAT'S CHEESE

2 TABLESPOONS VEGETABLE OIL

100 GRAMS TATSOI GREENS, WASHED
  AND PATTED DRY

Riesling Sauce

1 TEASPOON VEGETABLE OIL

1 TABLESPOON ONION, FINELY CHOPPED

200 ML RIESLING

¼ TEASPOON SUGAR

SALT AND WHITE PEPPER TO TASTE

2 TOMATOES, PEELED, SEEDED AND DICED

1 TABLESPOON BUTTER, CHILLED

RAVIOLI

Make sure the yabbie meat and egg white are very cold.

Place in a food processor or blender and pulse (do not over-process or the mixture will curdle). Season to taste.

Divide the mixture evenly between 12 wonton wrappers, spooning it onto the centre of each one.

Dot with a little goat's cheese.

Moisten the edges of the pastry, then top each one with another pastry wrapper and seal the edges to make ravioli.

Pan-fry in a little hot oil until the ravioli is golden and crispy on both sides.

RIESLING SAUCE

Sauté the onion in a little oil; cook until it is soft but not browned.

Add the white wine, sugar and seasoning.

Cook for 2 minutes to reduce and release the alcohol.

Remove from the heat and add the diced tomatoes.

Whisk in the butter.

To serve, place three ravioli on each plate. Divide the tatsoi leaves on top and surround with the riesling sauce.

CRISPED YABBIE *and* GOAT'S CHEESE RAVIOLI *with* TATSOI GREENS *and a* RIESLING SAUCE

GRILLED SCALLOPS
with GOAT'S CHEESE and PESTO

Scallops

12 SCALLOPS, OPENED, IN THE SHELL

12 TEASPOONS FRESH SOFT GOAT'S CHEESE

6 TEASPOONS PESTO SAUCE (SEE RECIPE ON THIS PAGE)

FRESHLY GROUND BLACK PEPPER

Pesto Sauce

1 BUNCH BASIL LEAVES, ROUGHLY TORN

¼ TEASPOON ROCK SALT

2–4 CLOVES GARLIC, PEELED AND ROUGHLY CHOPPED

¼ CUP PINE NUTS

4 TABLESPOONS BEST QUALITY PARMESAN CHEESE, FRESHLY GRATED

250 ML VIRGIN OLIVE OIL

SCALLOPS

Preheat the griller to very hot.

Place the scallops under the griller, still in their shells, and cook for 1–2 minutes.

Top each scallop with a teaspoon of goat's cheese and a little pesto.

Season with pepper and place under the griller again until the goat's cheese is lightly coloured.

Serve immediately.

Notes: The timing will depend on the heat range of the griller and the distance of the grill tray from the heat.

Take special care not to overcook the scallops as they shrink and become tough. As soon as they become opaque they are cooked.

PESTO SAUCE

Place all the ingredients except the oil in a food processor or blender.

Blend to a smooth paste.

Gradually add the oil, pouring in a steady stream.

GRILLED SCALLOPS *with* GOAT'S CHEESE *and* PESTO

CRISPY MORETON BAY BUG PARCELS

VEGETABLE OIL TO BRUSH MOULDS

16 SMALL SPRING-ROLL PASTRY
  WRAPPERS

12 LARGE RAW MORETON BAY BUGS,
  SHELLS REMOVED AND DEVEINED

2 TABLESPOONS VEGETABLE OIL

50 GRAMS BUTTON MUSHROOMS,
  THINLY SLICED

1 TABLESPOON LEMON JUICE

1 TABLESPOON WHITE WINE

1 TABLESPOON FISH SAUCE

1 TEASPOON SUGAR

SALT AND PEPPER TO TASTE

Brush four dariole moulds or ramekins with a little oil. Lay four spring-roll wrappers into each mould, leaving an overlap to cover the filling. Make sure there are no gaps at the bottom or sides of the moulds.

Clean the bug tails thoroughly. Pan-fry in 1 tablespoon of hot oil for 2 minutes (do not overcook). Remove from the pan and put aside.

In a clean frypan, sauté the mushrooms in the remaining 1 tablespoon of oil until the juices have evaporated. Add the lemon juice, white wine, fish sauce and sugar, and season to taste.

Combine with the bug meat, then distribute the mixture evenly between the four moulds.

Fold over the overlapping spring-roll wrappers and bake the moulds in a hot oven at 220°C for 8–10 minutes until golden and crispy. Unmould onto individual plates and serve immediately.

Delicious with Ginger and White Wine Sauce or Light Curry Sauce (see page 157).

STEAMED CRAB WITH BALSAMIC VINEGAR

4 WHOLE FRESH MUD CRABS

5 TABLESPOONS BALSAMIC VINEGAR

1 TABLESPOON OLIVE OIL

Freeze the crabs for 1 hour to put them to sleep.

Place them in a steamer over boiling water. Cover and steam for 10–15 minutes or until the crabs are cooked (the time needed will vary according to the size of the crabs).

Remove from the heat and allow to cool slightly.

Remove the top shell, cut each crab in half and clean the intestinal sac. Rinse. Crack the claws.

Heat the olive oil in a small saucepan until hot and add the balsamic vinegar. Stir to combine.

Pour the hot dressing over the crabs or use as a dipping sauce.

Note: This is Kenneth's favourite way of preparing crab, lobster or bugs as it retains all the original flavours and juices.

CHAR-GRILLED KING PRAWNS
with ROCKET *and* CRISPY RICE CAKE

2 TABLESPOONS ONION, FINELY CHOPPED

1 TABLESPOON OLIVE OIL

12 TABLESPOONS COOKED ARBORIO RICE

2 TABLESPOONS WHITE WINE

2 TABLESPOONS BEST QUALITY PARMESAN
  CHEESE, SHAVED

SALT AND PEPPER TO TASTE

VEGETABLE OIL FOR FRYING

2 TABLESPOONS VEGETABLE OIL

4 CLOVES GARLIC, WHOLE, PEELED

1 TABLESPOON WHITE WINE VINEGAR

2 CUPS FISH STOCK (SEE PAGE 153)

1 TABLESPOON FRESH TARRAGON LEAVES,
  CHOPPED

20 GREEN KING PRAWNS, SHELLS
  REMOVED

1 TABLESPOON BUTTER

2 BUNCHES FRESH ROCKET LEAVES

RICE CAKE

Sauté the onion in hot oil until soft.

Add the cooked rice and white wine; stir well.

Remove from the heat, season and stir in the Parmesan cheese.

Allow to cool, then shape into four cakes.

Pan-fry the rice cakes in a little hot oil on each side until crisp.

Keep warm.

SAUCE

Heat 2 tablespoons of oil and sauté the garlic cloves over medium heat until they change colour.

Drain off the oil and add the white wine vinegar, fish stock and tarragon.

Reduce to half a cup.

PRAWNS

Char-grill the prawns.

Heat the butter in a large frypan and quickly sauté the rocket until just wilted.

TO ASSEMBLE

Place each rice cake on a plate, then top with the rocket, distributing it evenly.

Spoon over the sauce and arrange five prawns on each stack.

CHAR-GRILLED KING PRAWNS
with STIR-FRIED VEGETABLES

20 LARGE GREEN PRAWNS, SHELLED
  AND DEVEINED

1 SMALL EGGPLANT, CUT INTO BATONS

4 TABLESPOONS PLAIN FLOUR

OIL FOR DEEP FRYING

1 TEASPOON VEGETABLE OIL

1 TEASPOON SESAME OIL

1 LARGE ZUCCHINI, CUT INTO BATONS

100 GRAMS BABY GREEN BEANS,
  TOPPED AND TAILED

150 GRAMS OYSTER MUSHROOMS,
  CUT IN HALF LENGTHWISE

1 WHOLE FRESH CHILLI, SEEDS REMOVED,
  AND CUT IN HALF

1 TEASPOON GARLIC, FINELY CHOPPED

2 TABLESPOONS WHITE WINE

¼ BUNCH FRESH CHIVES, CUT IN HALF
  LENGTHWISE

SALT AND PEPPER TO TASTE

Char-grill the prawns until they just change colour.

Remove from the heat and put aside.

Roll the eggplant batons in flour, shaking off the excess.

Heat the oil in a wok and deep-fry the eggplant until it is golden brown.

Remove with a slotted spoon and drain on paper towels.

In a clean wok, heat the vegetable oil and sesame oil and sauté the zucchini, beans, mushrooms, chilli and garlic for 2 minutes.

Add the eggplant and white wine, then toss to reheat.

Add the prawns and chives, season and toss to combine.

Remove the chilli and serve.

CHAR-GRILLED OCTOPUS *with a* BLACK-BEAN CAKE, ASPARAGUS *and* GARLIC *and* GINGER STOCK

200 GRAMS DRIED BLACK BEANS

1 TABLESPOON BUTTER

1 TABLESPOON ONION, FINELY CHOPPED

½ CUP WHITE WINE

1 TEASPOON SWEET PAPRIKA

2 TABLESPOONS CORIANDER LEAVES, CHOPPED

1 POTATO, STEAMED, PEELED AND MASHED

SALT AND PEPPER TO TASTE

1 TABLESPOON VEGETABLE OIL FOR FRYING

8 BABY OCTOPUS, HEADS REMOVED

OLIVE OIL FOR BRUSHING OCTOPUS

1 TEASPOON SUGAR

1 BUNCH FRESH ASPARAGUS

250 ML GARLIC AND GINGER STOCK (SEE PAGE 154)

4 TABLESPOONS SOUR CREAM

BLACK-BEAN CAKE

Soak the beans in water overnight; drain.

Simmer the beans in water until soft and open; drain.

Place in a bowl and mash well.

Sauté the onion in butter until soft; add the white wine and cook until reduced by half.

Add the black-bean mash, sweet paprika, coriander, mashed potato and seasoning.

Cook until quite dry.

Remove from the saucepan and allow to cool.

Shape the mixture into four cakes and pan-fry in oil until crispy. Keep hot.

OCTOPUS

Brush the octopus with olive oil.

Char-grill the octopus for 3–5 minutes, sprinkle with sugar and return to the grill for 1 minute.

ASPARAGUS

Steam or poach the asparagus for 2 minutes.

To serve, place the black-bean cakes on warmed plates, sit two octopus on top of each cake and garnish with asparagus.

Pour a little Garlic and Ginger Stock over and around the octopus.

Serve with sour cream.

CHAR-GRILLED OCTOPUS *with a* BLACK-BEAN CAKE, ASPARAGUS *and* GARLIC *and* GINGER STOCK

CHAR-GRILLED OCTOPUS *with* BLACK-EYE BEANS, SPINACH, BEAN SPROUTS *and* YOGHURT DRESSING

8 WHOLE BABY OCTOPUS, HEADS REMOVED

2 TABLESPOONS OLIVE OIL

1 TABLESPOON LIGHT SOY SAUCE

1 TEASPOON SUGAR

1 BUNCH SPINACH, WASHED, STEMS
REMOVED

100 GRAMS BEAN SHOOTS

1 TABLESPOON OLIVE OIL

$\frac{1}{2}$ TEASPOON BLACK PEPPER, COARSELY
GROUND

SALT TO TASTE

50 GRAMS BLACK-EYE BEANS, SOAKED
OVERNIGHT, SIMMERED FOR 30 MINUTES
OR UNTIL TENDER, THEN DRAINED

Yoghurt Dressing

125 GRAMS SHEEP'S MILK YOGHURT

250 GRAMS NATURAL YOGHURT

150 ML OLIVE OIL

$\frac{1}{2}$ TABLESPOON DIJON MUSTARD

$\frac{1}{4}$ TEASPOON GARLIC, FINELY CHOPPED

50 GRAMS SUGAR

1 TEASPOON LEMON JUICE

SALT AND PEPPER

OCTOPUS

Combine the oil, soy sauce and sugar.

Add the octopus and leave to marinate for at least 30 minutes.

Char-grill for 4–5 minutes.

YOGHURT DRESSING

Mix all the ingredients for the yoghurt dressing and whisk thoroughly to combine.

To serve, divide the spinach between four plates, then place two octopus on each plate.

Toss the bean shoots in oil, black pepper and salt, then place over the octopus.

Spoon over a little yoghurt sauce and sprinkle the black-eye beans around the plate.

WOK-SAUTÉED MUSSELS
with BLACK PEPPER and CHILLI SAUCE

Mussels

48 BLACK MUSSELS, SHELLS SCRUBBED
AND BEARDS REMOVED

1 ONION, FINELY DICED

1 CLOVE GARLIC, FINELY CHOPPED

1 CUP WHITE WINE

1 CUP WATER

Sauce

2 TABLESPOONS OLIVE OIL

½ ONION, FINELY CHOPPED

1 CLOVE GARLIC, FINELY CHOPPED

1 RED CHILLI, SEEDED AND FINELY
CHOPPED

1 TABLESPOON COARSELY GROUND
BLACK PEPPER

2 TABLESPOONS PLAIN FLOUR

2 CUPS MUSSEL LIQUOR

1 CUP RED WINE

1 TABLESPOON TOMATO PASTE

1 TEASPOON FRESH TARRAGON LEAVES,
CHOPPED

1 BAYLEAF

SALT TO TASTE

MUSSELS

Place the cleaned mussels in a large pot and
add the onion, garlic, white wine and water.

Cover and place over high heat.

Bring to the boil, shaking the pot until all
the mussels are opened (discard any that do
not open).

Lift out the mussels with a slotted spoon and
put aside.

Strain the juices, carefully avoiding any sand
at the bottom of the pot.

Measure to 2 cups; keep warm.

SAUCE

Heat the oil in a saucepan over medium heat.

Add the onion, garlic, chilli and black pepper;
sauté until soft but not browned.

Add the flour and stir well.

Whisk in the warm mussel juice, continuing
to whisk until smooth.

Add the red wine, tomato paste, tarragon,
bayleaf and seasoning.

Simmer over medium heat until the liquid is
reduced to 2 cups.

Add the mussels to the pan and toss well to
heat through.

Serve immediately with lots of crusty bread.

WOK-SAUTÉED
SQUID DUMPLINGS *in* LIGHT CURRY SAUCE

200 GRAMS SQUID TUBES, CLEANED AND
 MINCED

50 GRAMS SQUID TUBES, DICED

2 TABLESPOONS FLAT-LEAF PARSLEY,
 FINELY CHOPPED

1 BUNCH CORIANDER LEAVES, FINELY
 CHOPPED

1 TEASPOON PAPRIKA

1 TEASPOON SUGAR

2 TABLESPOONS WHITE WINE

1 TABLESPOON BRANDY

½ TEASPOON BLACK PEPPER, CRUSHED

SALT TO TASTE

2 EGG WHITES, LIGHTLY BEATEN

2 TABLESPOONS CORNFLOUR

2 CUPS VEGETABLE OIL FOR FRYING

Garnish

300 ML LIGHT CURRY SAUCE
 (SEE PAGE 157)

½ BUNCH WATERCRESS, WASHED,
 STALKS REMOVED

Make sure all the ingredients are cold.

Combine all the ingredients except for the oil for frying, adding the egg whites and cornflour last.

Using two tablespoons, shape the mixture into dumplings.

Place them on baking or parchment paper.

Heat the oil in a wok until it is very hot.

Deep-fry the dumplings a few at a time, turning once, until the outsides are golden and crispy. (Do not overcook.)

Place the dumplings on paper towels to drain.

In a clean saucepan, gently heat the Light Curry Sauce.

Add the dumplings and simmer for 4–5 minutes, coating the dumplings with the sauce.

Add the watercress, toss to wilt slightly, and remove from the heat.

Serve on four warm plates.

WOK-SAUTÉED SQUID DUMPLINGS *in* LIGHT CURRY SAUCE

SEARED SEA SCALLOPS *with* MIXED MUSHROOMS, POTATO CAKE *and* MULATO PEPPER

12 SEA SCALLOPS, LARGE

1 MULATO (BLACK) PEPPER, CHOPPED

1 TEASPOON OLIVE OIL

500 GRAMS PINK-EYE POTATOES, PEELED
  AND SLICED VERY FINELY

1 TEASPOON GARLIC, FINELY CHOPPED

½ TEASPOON SALT

½ TEASPOON BLACK PEPPER, COARSELY
  GROUND

1 TABLESPOON OLIVE OIL

2 TABLESPOONS FLOUR

1 TEASPOON BUTTER, MELTED

1 TABLESPOON OLIVE OIL

1 TABLESPOON ONION, FINELY CHOPPED

1 MULATO PEPPER, CHOPPED

4 OYSTER MUSHROOMS

4 SWISS (BROWN) MUSHROOMS

4 CHESTNUT MUSHROOMS

2 TABLESPOONS WHITE WINE

½ CUP FISH STOCK (SEE PAGE 153)

SALT AND PEPPER TO TASTE

½ TEASPOON SUGAR

1 TEASPOON BUTTER

Combine the scallops, mulato pepper and oil. Leave to marinate for 30 minutes.

POTATO CAKE

Toss the potato slices with the garlic, salt, black pepper and 1 tablespoon of olive oil.

Sprinkle with the flour, making sure it is evenly distributed.

Line a baking tray with baking paper.

Lay the potatoes on top, to an even thickness of approximately 2 cm.

Cover with another sheet of baking paper and bake in a hot oven at 200°C for 45 minutes.

Allow to cool, remove the baking paper and cut into four rounds.

Brush with the melted butter and bake in a hot oven at 200°C for 10–12 minutes.

Heat a wok until hot and sear the marinated scallops on all sides (2 minutes maximum). Take care not to overcook.

Put the scallops aside.

Sauté the onion in 1 tablespoon hot olive oil until soft; add the mulato pepper.

Add all the mushrooms and sauté for 1 minute.

Add the white wine, fish stock, seasoning and sugar.

Simmer until the mushrooms are soft.

Swirl in the butter.

Add the scallops and quickly toss to heat through.

To serve, place a hot potato cake on each plate; top with the scallops and mushrooms.

Notes: Dried mulato pepper is available in good delicatessens.

Button or enoki mushrooms may be used but will not give the same intensity of flavour.

SEARED SEA SCALLOPS *with* MIXED MUSHROOMS, POTATO CAKE *and* MULATO PEPPER

CHAR-GRILLED MORETON BAY BUGS MARINATED *in* CAJUN SPICES *with* SHIITAKE MUSHROOMS *and* ASPARAGUS

1 TABLESPOON OLIVE OIL

1 TABLESPOON CAJUN PASTE
  (SEE PAGE 169)

20 FRESH MORETON BAY BUG TAILS,
  HEADS OFF, SHELLS ON

1 TABLESPOON OLIVE OIL

1 TABLESPOON FRENCH ESCHALOTS,
  FINELY CHOPPED

20 SHIITAKE MUSHROOMS, WHOLE

1 BUNCH FRESH ASPARAGUS, CLEANED,
  CUT INTO 5 CM PIECES

1 TABLESPOON CAJUN PASTE

2 TABLESPOONS WHITE WINE

½ CUP FISH STOCK (SEE PAGE 153)

1 TEASPOON SUGAR

SALT AND PEPPER TO TASTE

1 TABLESPOON BUTTER

Combine the olive oil with the Cajun Paste; add the bugs and leave them to marinate for at least 10 minutes.

Char-grill the bugs on high heat, shell side down, until the shell changes colour.

Turn and grill the undersides for approximately 1 minute.

Remove from the heat and put aside.

Heat the olive oil in a large frypan and sauté the eschalots until they are soft.

Add the mushrooms and cook for 1 minute.

Add the asparagus and sauté for 1 minute.

Add the Cajun Paste; stir to release the aromas.

Add the bugs, white wine, fish stock and sugar; season then cook for 2 minutes.

Swirl in the butter and serve.

CHAR-GRILLED MORETON BAY BUGS MARINATED *in* CAJUN SPICES *with* SHIITAKE MUSHROOMS *and* ASPARAGUS

WOK-SAUTÉED MORETON BAY BUGS

with OKRA *and* ANCHO PEPPER

1 TABLESPOON BUTTER

1 TABLESPOON ONION, FINELY CHOPPED

1 TABLESPOON LEMONGRASS, FINELY CHOPPED

100 GRAMS DRIED BUTTER BEANS, SOAKED IN HOT WATER OVERNIGHT, SKINS REMOVED

2 TABLESPOONS WHITE WINE

1 CUP FISH STOCK (SEE PAGE 153)

12 FRESH MORETON BAY BUG TAILS, SHELLS REMOVED

1 TABLESPOON OLIVE OIL

1 TABLESPOON BUTTER

200 GRAMS FRESH OKRA, TRIMMED AND CUT IN HALF LENGTHWISE

2 DRIED ANCHO PEPPERS, FINELY CHOPPED

1 TEASPOON LEMON JUICE

1/2 TEASPOON SUGAR

SALT AND PEPPER TO TASTE

Heat the butter in a saucepan.

Add the onion and lemongrass and sauté until they are soft.

Add the butter beans, wine and fish stock.

Cover and simmer until the beans are tender (approximately 20 minutes).

Remove the mixture from the heat and leave the beans in their juices.

Heat the olive oil in a wok until very hot.

Wok-sauté the bugs over high heat until they are medium-cooked (approximately 1 minute).

Remove the bugs from the pan.

Reserve the cooking liquid.

Heat the butter in a separate frypan.

Sauté the okra and ancho peppers until the okra is just tender.

Add the bugs and their juices, lemon juice, sugar and beans in their liquid.

Season and cook for a further 2 minutes.

Serve immediately on four warm plates.

WOK-SAUTÉED MORETON BAY BUGS *with* OKRA *and* ANCHO PEPPER

STIR-FRIED MORETON BAY BUGS
in LEMONGRASS *and* MINT
with ZUCCHINI, EGG PASTRY *and* CHILLI JAM

1 TABLESPOON VEGETABLE OIL

20 MORETON BAY BUGS, HEADS AND
  SHELLS REMOVED

1 TABLESPOON VEGETABLE OIL

2 TABLESPOONS ONION, FINELY CHOPPED

1 TEASPOON FRENCH ESCHALOTS,
  FINELY CHOPPED

1 TABLESPOON LEMONGRASS,
  FINELY CHOPPED

2 ZUCCHINI, CUT LENGTHWISE INTO
  THIN RIBBONS

2 TABLESPOONS FRESH MINT LEAVES,
  CHOPPED

1 TEASPOON FLAT-LEAF PARSLEY, CHOPPED

2 TABLESPOONS WHITE WINE

½ CUP FISH STOCK (SEE PAGE 153)

SALT AND PEPPER TO TASTE

8 SHEETS EGG PASTRY (AVAILABLE
  AT CHINESE GROCERY SHOPS)

4 TABLESPOONS CHILLI JAM (SEE PAGE 166)

Heat the oil in a wok to very hot.

Stir-fry the bugs for 1 minute.

Remove and put aside with their juices.

In a clean wok, heat the oil; sauté the onion, eschalots and lemongrass until they are soft.

Add the zucchini and toss over heat until they are cooked but still firm.

Add the bugs with their juices, mint, parsley, white wine, fish stock and seasoning.

Stir over high heat for 1 minute.

Poach the egg pastry sheets in simmering water for 30 seconds, then drain.

TO ASSEMBLE

Set out four plates and place a egg pastry sheet on each one.

Divide the bug and zucchini mixture on top.

Top with another egg pastry sheet.

Spoon 1 tablespoon of Chilli Jam on each stack to create a 'hat' effect.

STIR-FRIED MORETON BAY BUGS *in* LEMONGRASS *and* MINT *with* ZUCCHINI, EGG PASTRY *and* CHILLI JAM

SEAFOOD XICHU

2 TABLESPOONS OLIVE OIL

200 GRAMS WHITE FISH FILLETS, CUT INTO
2 CM PIECES (SNAPPER OR OCEAN PERCH
ARE BOTH SUITABLE)

4 SCAMPI, SHELLS ON

16 BABY OCTOPUS, HEADS REMOVED

12 SCALLOPS

8 GREEN PRAWNS, SHELLS REMOVED

1 TABLESPOON OLIVE OIL

20 PIPIS, SOAKED IN COLD WATER FOR
30 MINUTES TO RELEASE SAND

1 TEASPOON FRENCH ESCHALOTS,
FINELY CHOPPED

3 FRESH CHILLIES, CUT IN HALF, SEEDS
REMOVED

40 SUGAR SNAP PEAS, TOPPED AND TAILED

4–6 TABLESPOONS XICHU PASTE
(AVAILABLE AT ASIAN GROCERY SHOPS)

2 TABLESPOONS WHITE WINE

1 TABLESPOON LEMON JUICE

1 CUP FISH STOCK (SEE PAGE 153)

½ TEASPOON SUGAR

Heat the olive oil in a wok.

Sauté the fish to seal it, then remove it with
a slotted spoon.

Sauté the scampi until the shells change
colour; remove.

Sauté the octopus for 3 minutes; remove.

Sauté the scallops to just seal; remove.

Sauté the prawns until they just change
colour; remove.

In a clean wok, heat the oil and sauté the
pipis, eschalots and chillies for 1 minute.

Add the sugar snap peas and toss briefly.

Add the xichu paste, white wine, lemon juice,
fish stock and sugar.

Bring to a simmer and add the seafood.

Cook for a further 2 minutes to finish cooking
the seafood.

Serve in four warm bowls.

Notes: Xichu paste is a spicy sauce made from
a base of dried scallops and dried prawns.

It is available in Asian grocery shops under
the Lee Kum Kee XO label.

Although relatively expensive, it can be used
to spice up many dishes.

It will spice up a pasta sauce and a few drops will
add wonderful complex flavours to seafood soup.

SEAFOOD XICHU

SCALLOP *and* OCEAN TROUT CARPACCIO
with WASABI DRESSING

500 GRAMS FRESH OCEAN TROUT FILLET,
  BONELESS, IN THE PIECE

20 SEA SCALLOPS OR BAY SCALLOPS,
  ROE REMOVED

Dressing

1 TABLESPOON WHITE WINE VINEGAR

3 TABLESPOONS OLIVE OIL

1/2 TEASPOON WASABI POWDER
  (AVAILABLE AT JAPANESE GROCERY
  SHOPS)

1 TEASPOON LIGHT SOY SAUCE

1 TEASPOON SAKE

1/2 TEASPOON SUGAR

Butterfly the trout, then flatten it gently with a rolling pin between two sheets of plastic wrap until it is an even thickness throughout.

Lay the scallops in a tight row in the centre of the trout.

Roll everything up tightly, avoiding air bubbles, and wrap it in foil.

Freeze until firm.

Whisk all the dressing ingredients together.

Defrost the trout and scallops slightly; cut it into very thin slices with a serrated knife.

To serve, overlap the slices on cold plates, arranging them in a circular pattern.

Drizzle the dressing over the top and serve immediately.

Note: Atlantic salmon may be substituted for the ocean trout.

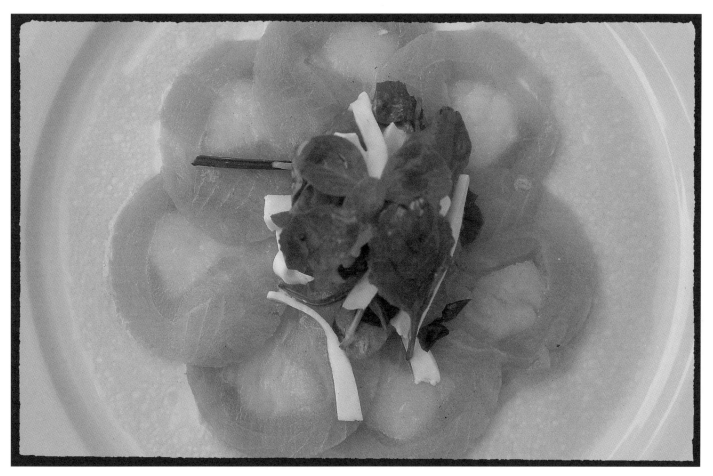

SCALLOP *and* OCEAN TROUT CARPACCIO *with* WASABI DRESSING

SAUTÉED LOBSTER *with* PEPPER *and* CHEESE SAUCE

4 SMALL WHOLE GREEN LOBSTER TAILS
 (BALMAIN OR MORETON BAY BUGS OR
 SCAMPI CAN BE SUBSTITUTED)

1 CUP CORNFLOUR

3 CUPS VEGETABLE OIL

1 TEASPOON BUTTER

1 TABLESPOON FRENCH ESCHALOTS

1 TABLESPOON BRANDY

½ CUP FISH STOCK (SEE PAGE 153)

300 ML WHITE PEPPER SAUCE
 (SEE PAGE 158)

1 TABLESPOON CHIVES, FINELY CHOPPED

2 TABLESPOONS BEST QUALITY PARMESAN
 CHEESE, FRESHLY SHAVED

Chop each lobster tail into four to six pieces.

Heat the oil in a wok to very hot.

Toss the lobster pieces in cornflour, shake off any excess and stir-fry, turning the pieces for 1–2 minutes until the shell changes colour.

If you are using a small wok, fry the lobster in two or three batches. Drain on paper towels.

In a frypan, heat the butter and sauté the eschalots until they are soft.

Add the brandy, fish stock and lobster. Toss well for 2 minutes.

Add the white pepper sauce and shaved Parmesan, stirring well to melt the cheese and coat the lobster.

Sprinkle over the chives and serve the lobster in a large bowl in the centre of the table, with plenty of napkins and finger bowls.

GRILLED BARRAMUNDI
with SQUID-INK PASTA, LIME *and* BASIL

100 GRAMS SQUID-INK PASTA
(AVAILABLE AT GOOD DELICATESSENS)

3 TABLESPOONS BUTTER

2 TABLESPOONS FRENCH ESCHALOTS,
FINELY CHOPPED

4 TABLESPOONS WHITE WINE

½ CUP FISH STOCK (SEE PAGE 153)

1 TABLESPOON FRESH BASIL LEAVES,
CUT INTO FINE STRIPS

2 TABLESPOONS OLIVE OIL

4 X 250 GRAMS BARRAMUNDI FILLETS,
SKIN LEFT ON AND CUT FROM THE
MIDDLE OF THE FISH

½ CUP CORNFLOUR

1 TEASPOON MELTED BUTTER

2 LIMES, PEELED AND SEGMENTED

4 TABLESPOONS CAVIAR OR SALMON
ROE FOR GARNISH

Cook the pasta in plenty of boiling water until *al dente*, then drain and put it aside.

Melt the butter in a frypan and sauté the eschalots until they are soft.

Add the white wine and fish stock and cook for 2 minutes.

Add the pasta and basil.

Toss gently to reheat.

Heat the olive oil in a frypan.

Dip the fish, skin side only, into the cornflour.

Shake off any excess.

Pan-fry, skin side down, in the hot oil, then reduce the heat and cook for approximately 2 minutes (the skin should be crispy).

Brush the top side of the fish with the melted butter and place it under a hot griller for 3 minutes.

Place two or three segments of lime on top and return the fish to the griller for 1 minute.

Divide the pasta into four bundles and place each one on a warm plate.

Garnish with the caviar.

Place the barramundi on top and spoon over any excess juices.

GRILLED BARRAMUNDI *with* SQUID-INK PASTA, LIME *and* BASIL

DEBONED BARRAMUNDI STUFFED *with* LEEKS

Fish

1 TABLESPOON OLIVE OIL

2 LEEKS, WHITE PART ONLY, WASHED WELL
AND CUT INTO THIN JULIENNE STRIPS

4 TABLESPOONS FLAT-LEAF PARSLEY,
CHOPPED

SALT AND PEPPER TO TASTE

4 X 300–350 GRAMS WHOLE FARMED
BARRAMUNDI, DEBONED FROM THE TOP,
DOWN THE BACK BONE
(A GOOD FISHMONGER WILL DO THIS)

½ CUP OLIVE OIL

½ CUP CORNFLOUR

Sauce

1 TABLESPOON OLIVE OIL

4 FRESH RED CHILLIES, CUT IN HALF,
SEEDS REMOVED

½ CUP FISH STOCK (SEE PAGE 153)

¼ CUP LIGHT SOY SAUCE

1 TABLESPOON SUGAR

1 BUNCH CORIANDER, LEAVES ONLY

FISH

Heat the olive oil in an ovenproof frypan and sauté the leeks until they are soft.

Remove from the heat and allow to cool.

Add the parsley and season.

Stuff the fish with the leek mixture.

Heat the oil in a large frypan.

Toss the fish in the cornflour, shaking off any excess, and fry for 1 minute on each side.

Place the pan in a hot oven at 200°C for 8–10 minutes.

Remove and place the fish under a hot griller for 1 minute to crisp the skin.

SAUCE

Heat the oil in a small saucepan and sauté the chilli for 15 seconds.

Add the fish stock, soy sauce and sugar.

Stir to combine.

Add the coriander, then remove the pan from the heat.

To serve, warm four plates and pour a little sauce on each one, taking care to divide the chillies equally.

Place a whole barramundi on each plate.

Note: Accompany with boiled potatoes and a simple salad.

BLUE-EYE COD FILLETS
with TOMATO, AVOCADO *and* BOCCONCINI SALSA

Fish

1 TABLESPOON OLIVE OIL

4 X 250 GRAMS BLUE-EYE COD FILLETS

1 TABLESPOON LEMON JUICE

1 TABLESPOON WORCESTERSHIRE SAUCE

1 TABLESPOON BUTTER, MELTED

Salsa

2 LARGE TOMATOES, PEELED, SEEDED
    AND DICED

½ ONION, FINELY DICED

2 TABLESPOONS CORIANDER LEAVES,
    CHOPPED

¼ CUP OLIVE OIL

1 TABLESPOON SUGAR

A FEW DROPS TABASCO SAUCE

SALT AND PEPPER TO TASTE

½ LARGE AVOCADO, DICED

50 GRAMS BOCCONCINI, MASHED

½ CUP FISH STOCK (SEE PAGE 153)

FISH

Heat the oil in a large ovenproof frypan over high heat until it is smoking hot.

Brush the fish fillets with the lemon juice and Worcestershire sauce.

Place the fish in the pan and sear it on both sides for 1 minute.

Transfer the pan to a hot oven and bake the fish at 200°C for 6–7 minutes.

(The time will vary according to the thickness of the fish.)

Remove from the oven, brush with the melted butter and place under a hot griller for 1 minute.

SALSA

Combine the tomatoes, onion, coriander, oil, sugar and Tabasco sauce.

Season to taste.

Fold in the avocado and bocconcini.

To serve, heat the fish stock.

Place the fish fillets on four warm plates.

Spoon over a little fish stock. Top with salsa.

PAN-FRIED SARDINES
with LAYERED VEGETABLES *and* SWEET OLIVE PASTE

Vegetables

2 RED CAPSICUMS

2 LARGE ZUCCHINI

1 EGGPLANT

250 GRAMS LARGE FLAT MUSHROOMS,
  STEMS REMOVED

8 LARGE CHINESE CABBAGE LEAVES

1 TABLESPOON OLIVE OIL

2 EGGS, LIGHTLY BEATEN

SALT AND PEPPER TO TASTE

Paste

125 GRAMS KALAMATA OLIVES, STONED

2 TABLESPOONS SWEET SOY SAUCE

2 TABLESPOONS OLIVE OIL

Fish

1 TABLESPOON OLIVE OIL

16 SARDINE FILLETS

1 TABLESPOON LEMON JUICE

2 TABLESPOONS WHITE WINE

¼ TEASPOON GROUND BLACK PEPPER

VEGETABLES

Char-grill the capsicums, remove their skins; cut into four lobes and remove the seeds.

Cut the zucchini and eggplant lengthwise into thin strips, then char-grill until they are coloured but firm.

Char-grill the mushrooms until they colour.

Poach or steam the Chinese cabbage until it is just wilted; drain and refresh. Dry on paper towels.

Brush a cake tin with olive oil.

Season the eggs with salt and pepper. Dip all the vegetables in the egg mixture. Place the vegetables in the oiled cake tin, beginning with a layer of capsicum, then adding the mushrooms, whole cabbage leaves, eggplant and zucchini, layer by layer.

Bake in the oven at 180°C for 45 minutes.

Cover with foil and bake for a further 20 minutes; allow to cool in the tin.

Turn out, leaving the capsicum on top, and cut into four.

Reheat, loosely covered in foil, for 15 minutes in a moderate oven (180°C).

PASTE

In a food processor or blender, process the olives, soy sauce and olive oil to a paste.

FISH

Heat the olive oil in a large frypan.

Wash and dry the sardine fillets.

Combine the lemon juice, wine and pepper. Dip the sardines in this mixture, then pan-fry them for 30 seconds on each side.

To serve, place a portion of layered vegetables on warm plates.

Arrange four sardine fillets on each and top with a tablespoon of sweet olive paste.

PAN-FRIED SARDINES *with* LAYERED VEGETABLES *and* SWEET OLIVE PASTE

POACHED ATLANTIC SALMON
with OYSTERS *and* VEGETABLES *in* BROTH

4 X 200 GRAMS ATLANTIC SALMON FILLETS

Court Bouillon
2 LITRES WATER
200 ML WHITE WINE
1 ONION, ROUGHLY CHOPPED
1 CARROT, PEELED AND CHOPPED
3 PARSLEY STALKS
1 BAYLEAF
1 SPRIG FRESH THYME
12 WHOLE BLACK PEPPERCORNS
1 TABLESPOON SALT

Broth
1 TEASPOON OLIVE OIL
1 LEEK, WHITE PART ONLY, WASHED WELL
   AND FINELY SLICED
1 PUNNET OYSTER MUSHROOMS
½ CUP WHITE WINE
6 CUPS FISH STOCK (SEE PAGE 153)
1 SPRIG FRESH THYME
2 LARGE RIPE TOMATOES, SKINNED,
   SEEDED AND DICED
1 BUNCH ENGLISH SPINACH LEAVES,
   WASHED AND STEMS REMOVED
12 OYSTERS
2 TABLESPOONS FRESH CORIANDER LEAVES

COURT BOUILLON

Place all the ingredients for the court bouillon in a large saucepan.

Simmer for 30 minutes then strain.

In a clean saucepan, bring the court bouillon to a simmer.

Add the salmon fillets, return to a simmer, then cover and turn off the heat.

Leave for 5 minutes.

Remove the salmon fillets and place them in four warm soup plates.

BROTH

Heat the olive oil in a large saucepan and sauté the leeks until they are soft.

Add the mushrooms; sauté for 2 minutes.

Add the white wine and bring to a simmer.

Add the fish stock and thyme.

Simmer for 2 minutes.

Add the diced tomatoes and spinach leaves, return the mixture to a simmer, then remove it from the heat.

Add the oysters and coriander leaves.

Spoon the broth equally over the salmon fillets and serve.

POACHED ATLANTIC SALMON *with* OYSTERS *and* VEGETABLES *in* BROTH

PAN-FRIED TUNA FILLETS
in PAPRIKA *and* OLIVE OIL
with WOK-SAUTÉED POTATOES *and* MUSHROOMS

2 TABLESPOONS SWEET PAPRIKA

½ TEASPOON CHILLI POWDER

1 TEASPOON SUGAR

¼ CUP OLIVE OIL

4 X 250 GRAMS TUNA FILLETS

2 CUPS VEGETABLE OIL FOR FRYING

4 POTATOES, PEELED AND CUT INTO
   THIN SLICES

2 TABLESPOONS OLIVE OIL

1 TEASPOON FRENCH ESCHALOTS,
   FINELY CHOPPED

50 GRAMS SMALL BUTTON MUSHROOMS

75 GRAMS OYSTER MUSHROOMS

1 TEASPOON DIJON MUSTARD

1 CUP FISH STOCK (SEE PAGE 153)

1 TABLESPOON WHITE WINE

1 TEASPOON LEMON JUICE

50 ENOKI MUSHROOMS

1 TABLESPOON CHIVES, FINELY CHOPPED

JUICE OF ½ LEMON

SALT AND PEPPER TO TASTE

Combine the paprika, chilli powder, sugar and oil. Add the tuna and leave to marinate for 30 minutes.

Heat the vegetable oil in a wok and stir-fry the potato slices for 3–4 minutes.

Drain on kitchen paper.

Heat the olive oil in a large frypan and sauté the eschalots until they are soft.

Add the button and oyster mushrooms and sauté for 2 minutes.

Add the potatoes and toss to heat.

Mix the Dijon mustard, fish stock, white wine and lemon juice.

Add to the pan.

Add the enoki mushrooms and chives.

Do not overcook.

Heat a frypan over a medium heat.

Remove the tuna from the marinade.

Sprinkle with the lemon juice, add seasoning and pan-fry on each side for 1 ½ minutes.

(It is important that the frypan is not too hot or it will scorch the paprika, making it bitter. The tuna should be rare in the middle.)

To serve, distribute the vegetables evenly between four warm soup plates and place the tuna on top. Garnish with enoki mushrooms.

PAN-FRIED TUNA FILLETS *in* PAPRIKA *and* OLIVE OIL *with* WOK-SAUTÉED POTATOES *and* MUSHROOMS

KING GEORGE WHITING FILLETS
with SORREL *and* TARO NOODLES

Sauce

1 TABLESPOON OLIVE OIL

2 TABLESPOONS ONION, FINELY CHOPPED

1 TEASPOON LEMONGRASS, FINELY
  CHOPPED

½ CUP WATER

4 TABLESPOONS JIMMY'S SATÉ SAUCE
  (AVAILABLE AT ASIAN GROCERY SHOPS)

2 TEASPOONS SWEET SOY SAUCE

1 TEASPOON BUTTER

Noodles

320 GRAMS JAPANESE TARO NOODLES
  (AVAILABLE AT ASIAN GROCERY SHOPS)

1 TABLESPOON OLIVE OIL

1 BUNCH FRESH SORREL LEAVES

½ CUP FISH STOCK (SEE PAGE 153)

Fish

½ CUP VEGETABLE OIL

1 LEMON, CUT IN HALF

12 KING GEORGE WHITING FILLETS

½ CUP CORNFLOUR

SALT AND PEPPER TO TASTE

SAUCE

Heat the olive oil and sauté the onion and lemongrass until they are soft.

Add the water, saté sauce and soy sauce.

Bring to the boil and turn off the heat.

Whisk in the butter.

NOODLES

Drain the liquid from the noodles and rinse in clean water two or three times. Put aside.

FISH

Heat the oil in a large frypan to very hot.

Squeeze the lemon juice over the whiting fillets.

Dip them in cornflour and shake off any excess.

Place the whiting fillets, skin side down, in the hot oil.

Cook for 1 minute. Turn and cook the other side for 1 minute.

Remove with a slotted spoon and drain on paper towels.

Season to taste.

In a clean pan, heat the olive oil and sauté the sorrel leaves until they begin to wilt.

Add the taro noodles and toss.

Add the saté sauce mixture and fish stock.

Cook for 1 minute.

To serve, divide the sorrel and noodles between four warm plates. Place the whiting fillets on top.

Note: Jimmy's Saté Sauce is essential to this dish. It is quite unlike the saté sauce typically seen in Thai or Malaysian cooking.

KING GEORGE WHITING FILLETS *with* SORREL *and* TARO NOODLES

GRILLED SWORDFISH
with SPICY SUMMER VEGETABLES

Vegetables

2 CUPS VEGETABLE OIL

1 MEDIUM EGGPLANT, CUT INTO
  LARGE DICE

½ CUP FLOUR

½ LARGE WHITE ONION, CUT INTO
  LARGE DICE

1 LARGE ZUCCHINI, CUT INTO LARGE DICE

100 GRAMS BUTTON MUSHROOMS CUT IN
  QUARTERS

2 TABLESPOONS TOMATO PASTE

1 TEASPOON SWEET PAPRIKA

½ TEASPOON SUGAR

SALT AND PEPPER TO TASTE

½ CUP FISH STOCK (SEE PAGE 153)

Fish

1 TABLESPOON WORCESTERSHIRE SAUCE

1 TEASPOON LEMON JUICE

4 X 250 GRAMS SWORDFISH CUTLETS

1 TABLESPOON OLIVE OIL

1 TABLESPOON BUTTER, MELTED

VEGETABLES

Heat the oil in a wok to very hot.

Toss the eggplant in the flour, shaking off any excess.

Fry in hot oil until the eggplant is coloured.

Remove with a slotted spoon and drain on paper towels.

Drain off all but 1 tablespoon of oil from the wok.

Return the heat to medium and sauté the onion until it is clear and soft.

Add the zucchini and sauté for 1 minute.

Add the mushrooms and sauté for a further 2 minutes.

Add the eggplant, tomato paste, sweet paprika, sugar and seasoning.

Toss quickly to combine.

FISH

Combine the Worcestershire sauce and lemon juice.

Brush both sides of the fish with this mixture.

Heat the oil in a large frypan and sear each side of the fish.

Brush the top side with the melted butter.

Place under a hot griller for 2 minutes.

Heat the fish stock.

To serve, arrange the swordfish cutlets on four warm plates.

Divide the vegetables on top.

Spoon the fish stock over the vegetables and serve.

GRILLED SWORDFISH *with* SPICY SUMMER VEGETABLES

STEAMED WHOLE BABY SNAPPER
with SOY *and* GINGER

2 TEASPOONS GARLIC, FINELY CHOPPED

2 TABLESPOONS GINGER, PEELED AND
CUT INTO FINE JULIENNE STRIPS

4 WHOLE BABY SNAPPER, CLEANED

1 BUNCH CORIANDER, LEAVES ONLY

2 SPRING ONIONS, CUT INTO THIN
JULIENNE STRIPS

8 TABLESPOONS LIGHT SOY SAUCE

1 CUP VEGETABLE OIL

This recipe requires a steamer-basket that can hold the fish on a large plate with enough room around the sides to allow the steam to rise evenly.

Spread the garlic and ginger over the top of each fish.

Place on a large plate in a steamer-basket.

Cover and steam over simmering water for 10 minutes.

Remove from the heat and divide the coriander and spring onions over the fish.

Pour 2 tablespoons of soy sauce over each fish.

Heat the oil to smoking and carefully pour over each fish, pouring from head to tail.

Note: This is an extremely simple and delicious recipe that is suitable for any fish or fillets. Adjust the cooking time if using fillets — salmon fillets will need to steam for only 3–4 minutes.

STEAMED WHOLE BABY SNAPPER *with* SOY *and* GINGER

MOONFISH *with* SWEET POTATOES
and TAMARILLO SAUCE

8 TAMARILLOS

1 CUP FISH STOCK (SEE PAGE 153)

2 TABLESPOONS WHITE WINE

1 TEASPOON LEMON JUICE

1 TEASPOON VINEGAR

3 TABLESPOONS SUGAR

½ CUP CASTER SUGAR

1 LARGE SWEET POTATO, PEELED
   AND THINLY SLICED

1 CUP VEGETABLE OIL

2 TEASPOONS BUTTER

1 TABLESPOON OLIVE OIL

1 LEMON, CUT IN HALF

8 X 100 GRAMS MOONFISH FILLETS
   (BLUE EYE COD, OCEAN PERCH OR
   JEWFISH ARE ALSO SUITABLE)

SALT AND PEPPER TO TASTE

TAMARILLOS

Place the tamarillos in boiling water for 2 minutes.

Drain and plunge into cold water, then remove the skins.

Reserve four tamarillos for garnish and use four for the sauce.

Cut four tamarillos into chunky pieces and place in a saucepan with the fish stock, white wine, lemon juice, vinegar and 3 tablespoons of sugar.

Place over a moderate heat and simmer until thick and reduced by half.

Roll the remaining four tamarillos in caster sugar and place them in an ovenproof frypan.

Place in a hot oven at 200°C until the sugar melts.

Shake the pan and place it under a hot griller to caramelise the sugar. Put aside.

SWEET POTATOES

Wok-fry the sweet potato slices in hot oil for approximately 2 minutes or until they are almost soft.

Drain on paper towels. Heat the butter in a frypan and sauté the potatoes, tossing until they are hot.

FISH

Heat 1 tablespoon of olive oil in a large frypan until it is very hot.

Squeeze the lemon juice over the fish and season.

Pan-fry each side for 1½ minutes.

To serve, glaze each plate with some sauce, place a ring of potatoes in the centre and top each one with two fish fillets.

Garnish with a whole caramelised tamarillo.

ATLANTIC SALMON
with WILD RICE *and* CHAMPAGNE SAUCE

½ CUP VEGETABLE OIL

½ CUP CASTER SUGAR

2 TABLESPOONS FRESH DILL, CHOPPED

4 X 250 GRAMS ATLANTIC SALMON FILLETS,
  CUT FROM THE CENTRE OF THE FISH

2 LIMES, PEELED AND CUT INTO
  THIN SLICES

Rice

1 TABLESPOON BUTTER

2 TABLESPOONS ONION, FINELY CHOPPED

2 CUPS COOKED WILD RICE

½ CUP WHITE WINE

½ CUP BEST QUALITY PARMESAN CHEESE,
  FRESHLY GRATED

SALT AND PEPPER TO TASTE

Champagne Sauce

1 TEASPOON BUTTER

1 TABLESPOON FRENCH ESCHALOTS,
  FINELY CHOPPED

1 CUP CHAMPAGNE

1 TABLESPOON WHITE WINE VINEGAR

½ CUP FISH STOCK (SEE PAGE 153)

½ TEASPOON SUGAR

SALT AND PEPPER TO TASTE

1 TABLESPOON BUTTER

FISH

Combine the oil, sugar and dill. Add the salmon. Leave to marinate for at least 2 hours, then strain, reserving the marinade.

Heat a large ovenproof frypan and cook the salmon for 2 minutes, spooning a little of the marinade over each fillet.

(Be careful not to burn the sugar.)

Remove from the heat.

Turn the fish over and dress it with slices of lime.

Place the pan in a hot oven at 200°C for 3–4 minutes. Remove.

RICE

Heat the butter and sauté the onion until soft.

Add the rice and white wine. Stir well to absorb the liquid.

Add the Parmesan cheese and season.

SAUCE

Heat butter and sauté the eschalots until soft.

Add the champagne and white wine vinegar.

Simmer and reduce to half a cup.

Add the fish stock and sugar.

Season to taste.

Cook for a further 2 minutes.

Remove from the heat and whisk in the butter.

To serve, warm four plates and pour a little sauce on each one.

Divide the rice in a pile on top, then lay over the salmon fillets.

ATLANTIC SALMON *with* WILD RICE *and* CHAMPAGNE SAUCE

WOK-FRIED FLOUNDER FILLETS *with* SHIITAKE MUSHROOMS, ASPARAGUS *and* SWEET CHILLI SAUCE

8 X 100 GRAMS FLOUNDER FILLETS, SKIN ON

½ CUP CORNFLOUR

2 CUPS VEGETABLE OIL, FOR FRYING

1 TABLESPOON FRENCH ESCHALOTS, FINELY CHOPPED

1 TABLESPOON OLIVE OIL

1 BUNCH ASPARAGUS, STEMS TRIMMED

100 GRAMS SHIITAKE MUSHROOMS

2 TABLESPOONS WHITE WINE

2 TABLESPOONS SWEET CHILLI SAUCE

½ CUP FISH STOCK (SEE PAGE 153)

1 TABLESPOON LEMON JUICE

SALT AND PEPPER TO TASTE

Cut each fish fillet lengthwise into three pieces.

Dip the fillets in the cornflour, shaking off any excess.

Heat the oil in a wok to very hot and fry the fillets for 2 minutes.

Remove with a slotted spoon and drain on paper towels.

In a frypan, sauté the eschalots in hot olive oil until they are soft.

Add the asparagus and sauté for 1 minute.

Add the shiitake mushrooms and sauté for 1 minute.

Add the white wine, sweet chilli sauce, fish stock and lemon juice.

Season.

Place the fish in the sauce and shake the pan for 30 seconds to coat the fish. Serve.

WOK-FRIED FLOUNDER FILLETS *with* SHIITAKE MUSHROOMS, ASPARAGUS *and* SWEET CHILLI SAUCE

JEWFISH *with* MACADAMIA NUTS *and* SPINACH
in MILK *and* GINGER BROTH

4 X 250 GRAMS JEWFISH FILLETS

1 TABLESPOON OLIVE OIL

1 TEASPOON BUTTER, MELTED

1/2 CUP MACADAMIA NUTS, CHOPPED
AND ROASTED

Broth

1 TEASPOON OLIVE OIL

1/2 LARGE ONION, CUT INTO FINE
JULIENNE STRIPS

5 CM PIECE GINGER, PEELED AND FINELY
SLICED

1 TEASPOON WHITE PEPPERCORNS,
LIGHTLY CRUSHED

1 BAYLEAF

1/2 CUP WHITE WINE

2 CUPS FISH STOCK (SEE PAGE 153)

2 CUPS MILK

1/4 TEASPOON SUGAR

SALT AND PEPPER TO TASTE

2 BUNCHES ENGLISH SPINACH,
LEAVES ONLY, WASHED WELL

Pan-fry the fish in hot oil for 1 1/2 minutes; turn, brush with melted butter and place in a hot oven at 200°C for 5 minutes.

Remove and brush with melted butter.

BROTH

Heat the oil and sauté the onion, ginger and pepper for 2 minutes.

Add the bayleaf, white wine and fish stock.

Cook for 2 minutes.

Add the milk; simmer until reduced to 2 cups.

Add the sugar and season to taste.

Strain into a clean pan, return to the heat and add the spinach until it is just wilting.

To serve, divide the broth between four warm soup plates, add the fish and sprinkle with the roasted macadamia nuts.

Jewfish *with* Macadamia Nuts *and* Spinach *in* Milk *and* Ginger Broth

Gum Leaf-Marinated Ocean Trout
with Fresh Egg Noodles
and Cherry Tomato Compote

1 DROP GUM LEAF OIL (AVAILABLE FROM
   BUSH TUCKER SUPPLIERS AND GOOD
   DELICATESSENS)

½ CUP VEGETABLE OIL

2 TABLESPOONS SUGAR

SALT AND PEPPER TO TASTE

4 X 120 GRAMS OCEAN TROUT FILLETS

250 GRAMS FRESH EGG NOODLES

2 TABLESPOONS BUTTER

SALT AND PEPPER TO TASTE

½ CUP FISH STOCK (SEE PAGE 153)

CHERRY TOMATO COMPOTE
   (SEE PAGE 168)

1 TABLESPOON FRESH CHIVES, FINELY
   CHOPPED

Combine the gum leaf oil, vegetable oil, sugar and seasoning. Add the trout and leave to marinate for 30 minutes. (Reserve the marinade.)

Cook the noodles in plenty of boiling, salted water for 4–5 minutes, until *al dente*.

Drain.

Heat the butter in a large frypan and sauté the noodles for 2 minutes.

Season to taste.

Heat 2 tablespoons of the marinade oil in a large heavy-based frypan over high heat until it is very hot.

Seal the trout on both sides for 1 minute.

Bring the fish stock to the boil.

Warm the Cherry Tomato Compote.

Divide the noodles onto four warm plates.

Top each one with a trout fillet.

Pour over a little of the hot fish stock and dress with Cherry Tomato Compote and a sprinkling of fresh chives.

SHIRAZ-GLAZED MUSCOVY DUCK BREASTS
with WILTED SPINACH *and a* POTATO CAKE

Potato Cake

300 GRAMS POTATOES, CUT INTO FINE
 JULIENNE STRIPS
1 MEDIUM WHITE ONION, GRATED
1 TEASPOON PLAIN FLOUR
SALT AND PEPPER TO TASTE
1 TABLESPOON BUTTER
1 TABLESPOON OIL

Spinach

1 BUNCH ENGLISH SPINACH LEAVES
1 TEASPOON OLIVE OIL

Duck Breasts

1 TABLESPOON OLIVE OIL
4 MUSCOVY DUCK BREASTS, PRE-ROASTED
 (SEE RECIPE, PAGE 171)

Shiraz Glaze

100 GRAMS SUGAR
500 ML SHIRAZ
PINCH OF SALT
SZECHUAN PEPPER, TO TASTE

POTATO CAKE

Mix the potato, onion, flour and seasoning.

Form into four round flat cakes.

Heat the butter and oil in a frypan and cook
on both sides until crisp and golden.

Remove, drain on paper towels and
keep warm.

SPINACH

Wash the spinach leaves in several changes
of cold water.

Shake off the excess moisture and sauté in hot
oil until just wilted. Remove and keep warm.

DUCK BREASTS

Sear on both sides in a little hot oil
(approximately 2 minutes per side).

Alternatively, place the breasts under a hot
griller for 2 minutes each side.

SHIRAZ GLAZE

Place the sugar in a heavy-based saucepan
and caramelise over high heat.

As soon as the sugar turns a deep golden
colour, carefully pour in the wine.

Stir to dissolve the sugar and reduce to
200 ml.

Season with salt and Szechuan pepper.

TO ASSEMBLE

Flood four plates with the shiraz glaze.

Place a potato cake in the centre of
each plate.

Divide the spinach over the potato cakes.

Fan each duck breast on top of the spinach
and sprinkle with Szechuan pepper.

SHIRAZ-GLAZED MUSCOVY DUCK BREASTS *with* WILTED SPINACH *and a* POTATO CAKE

DOUBLE-ROASTED MUSCOVY DUCK
with RED WINE JUS, CORN MASH and ORANGE GLAZE

2 X NO. 12 MUSCOVY DUCKS,
  PRE-ROASTED AS PER RECIPE PAGE 171

1 TABLESPOON OIL, RESERVED FROM
  PRE-ROASTING PROCESS

Jus

1 ONION, ROUGHLY CHOPPED

1 CARROT, ROUGHLY CHOPPED

1 STICK CELERY, ROUGHLY CHOPPED

10 WHOLE PEPPERCORNS

2 TABLESPOONS TOMATO PASTE

1 BAYLEAF

1 CUP RED WINE

1 CUP PORT

1 LITRE WATER

Orange Glaze

2 TEASPOONS HONEY

1 TEASPOON SUGAR

1 CUP ORANGE JUICE

1 TEASPOON EXTRA SUGAR

1 ORANGE, SEGMENTED (FOR GARNISH)

CORN MASH (SEE PAGE 171)

DUCK AND JUS

Cut the pre-roasted duck in half.

Remove the back bone and as many bones as possible from the cavity without damaging the shape.

Put aside the duck halves and reserve the bones for the sauce.

Place the reserved oil, onion, carrot, celery, peppercorns, tomato paste and bayleaf in a roasting dish.

Sauté over high heat for 2 minutes, then roast in a hot oven at 200°C for 30 minutes.

Remove from the oven and deglaze the pan with the wine and port.

Place the reserved duck bones, vegetables and wine in a clean saucepan, then add the water.

Simmer for 1 hour.

Strain and pour into a clean roasting dish.

Place the duck halves skin side up in the stock and roast at 200°C for 30 minutes.

Remove the duck and strain the jus, removing any fat.

ORANGE GLAZE

Cook together the honey, sugar and orange juice until the mixture is thick and syrupy.

Brush over the skin side of the ducks and sprinkle the extra sugar over the top.

Place under a hot griller for 2 minutes or until the sugar caramelises.

To serve, place each duck half on a little jus and accompany with a mound of Corn Mash.

Garnish with segmented orange.

DOUBLE-ROASTED MUSCOVY DUCK *with* RED WINE JUS, CORN MASH *and* ORANGE GLAZE

DUCK PARCELS *on* WILTED PAK CHOY

2 X NO. 12 DUCKS, PRE-ROASTED AS PER
  RECIPE ON PAGE 171

500 ML DUCK STOCK (PAGE 155)

250 ML GARLIC AND GINGER STOCK
  (PAGE 154)

1 CUP WHITE WINE

2 TEASPOONS GINGER, FINELY CHOPPED

1 TEASPOON BUTTER

16 WHOLE FRESHLY ROASTED CHESTNUTS

16 SMALL SPRING-ROLL WRAPPERS

1 TABLESPOON VEGETABLE OIL

2 BUNCHES PAK CHOY, TRIMMED AND
  WASHED WELL

DUCK

Remove the meat from the ducks and chop it
into pieces.

Place the meat in a roasting pan and pour
over the stocks.

Cover with foil and braise in the oven at
180°C for 30 minutes.

Remove the meat with a slotted spoon and
pour the stock into a saucepan to use as sauce.

Add the white wine and ginger.

Reduce to 250 ml.

Strain through a fine sieve.

Sauté the chestnuts in butter until they
colour.

Add to the duck with a little of the reduced
stock to just moisten.

Allow to cool.

Brush four dariole moulds with oil and
lay four spring-roll wrappers in each one,
overlapping the sheets so that the filling can
be covered.

Fill with the duck mixture and fold over the
overlapping wrappers. Brush with a little oil.

Place the moulds upside down on a baking
tray and bake in a hot oven at 200°C for
15 minutes.

Remove the parcels from the mould, then
return them to the oven for 5 minutes or until
the tops are crisp.

PAK CHOY

Blanch the pak choy in salted water until it is
just wilted, then drain.

To serve, warm four plates, pour a little duck
sauce on each one, arrange the pak choy and
carefully top with a duck parcel.

RABBIT *and* SAUTERNE PIE

Sauce

RABBIT BONES FROM 2 RABBITS

1 ONION, ROUGHLY CHOPPED

1 CARROT, ROUGHLY CHOPPED

1 STICK CELERY, ROUGHLY CHOPPED

2 BAYLEAVES

2 SPRIGS FRESH THYME

1 TEASPOON WHOLE PEPPERCORNS

500 ML SAUTERNE

500 ML CREAM

1 LITRE WATER

2 TEASPOONS ENGLISH MUSTARD

SALT AND PEPPER TO TASTE

2 WHOLE FARMED RABBITS, BONED AND
    CUT INTO LARGE DICE

½ CUP FLOUR

½ CUP OLIVE OIL

1 ONION, FINELY DICED

2 CARROTS, CUT INTO 1 CM DICE

2 STICKS CELERY, CUT INTO 1 CM DICE

2 POTATOES, CUT INTO 1 CM DICE

4 SHEETS PUFF PASTRY

1 WHOLE EGG, BEATEN

SAUCE

Roast the bones, onion, carrot and celery for 30 minutes in a hot oven at 220°C to colour.

Deglaze the pan with the wine.

Place the bones, vegetables, bayleaves, thyme, peppercorns, wine, cream and water in a large saucepan.

Simmer until the liquid is reduced to 500 ml.

Strain, add the mustard and season to taste.

RABBIT

Toss the rabbit pieces in flour, shaking off any excess.

Heat the oil in a large frypan and sauté the rabbit until it is sealed on all sides and lightly coloured.

Remove with a slotted spoon.

Drain off all but 1 tablespoon of the oil. Heat and sauté the onion, carrots, celery and potatoes for 3 minutes.

Add the rabbit and the sauce.

Gently simmer for 5 minutes.

Distribute the rabbit mixture between four ramekins.

Top with the pastry, brush with the beaten egg and bake in a hot oven at 220°C for 8–10 minutes or until browned.

Serve immediately with a salad of mixed leaves.

SPICY CORN-FED CHICKEN
with PROSCIUTTO *and* ARTICHOKE RISOTTO

Chicken

½ CUP VEGETABLE OIL

4 TABLESPOONS SOUR CREAM

2 TABLESPOONS LEMON JUICE

1 TABLESPOON SUGAR

1 TEASPOON SWEET PAPRIKA

½ TEASPOON CHILLI POWDER

¼ TEASPOON SALT

6 CORN-FED CHICKEN BREASTS,
   EACH CUT INTO FOUR STRIPS

Risotto

4 FRESH ARTICHOKES, CLEANED, FINELY
   SLICED AND PLACED IN ACIDULATED
   WATER TO AVOID BROWNING

4 TABLESPOONS BUTTER

2 TABLESPOONS ONION, FINELY DICED

1½ CUPS ARBORIO RICE

1 CUP WHITE WINE

4 CUPS CHICKEN STOCK (SEE PAGE 152)

1 CUP BEST QUALITY PARMESAN CHEESE,
   FRESHLY SHAVED

SALT AND FRESHLY GROUND BLACK
   PEPPER TO TASTE

8 VERY THIN SLICES PROSCIUTTO

CHICKEN

Combine the oil, sour cream, lemon juice, sugar, paprika, chilli powder and salt. Add the chicken strips and leave to marinate for at least 30 minutes.

RISOTTO

Drain and pat dry the artichoke slices.

Melt the butter and sauté the onion until it is soft and clear.

Add the rice and stir well to coat with butter.

Add the artichokes and sauté for 1 minute.

Add the white wine and stir until it is almost absorbed.

Slowly add the hot chicken stock, ladle by ladle, until the rice is firm but cooked.

(The risotto will continue to absorb the liquid when it is resting.)

Stir in the Parmesan cheese, season to taste.

Cover and leave to rest for 5 minutes.

Heat a large frypan over medium heat, then fry the chicken pieces on each side for approximately 2 minutes, taking care not to burn the spices.

(Fry in two or more batches if the pan is too small to hold all the pieces in one layer.)

Place the prosciutto under a hot griller until it is well crisped.

Drain on paper towels.

To serve, place a mound of risotto on four warm plates, top with the chicken and garnish with the crispy prosciutto.

Note: This chicken can also be cooked on the barbecue.

SPICY CORN-FED CHICKEN *with* PROSCIUTTO *and* ARTICHOKE RISOTTO

KANGAROO *with* ASIAN LEAF *and* PINK GRAPEFRUIT SALAD

1 TEASPOON LEMONGRASS,
  FINELY CHOPPED

1 CLOVE GARLIC, FINELY CHOPPED

½ TEASPOON CRUSHED BLACK PEPPER

400 GRAMS KANGAROO RUMP, CUT
  INTO 4 PIECES

1 TABLESPOON OLIVE OIL

Salad

½ BUNCH BOK CHOY, WASHED

½ BUNCH CHOY SUM, WASHED

½ BUNCH CHINESE BROCCOLI, WASHED

1 CUP TATSOI LEAVES, WASHED

2 PINK GRAPEFRUIT, PEELED AND
  SEGMENTED

Dressing

¼ CUP FRESH GRAPEFRUIT JUICE

2 TABLESPOONS OLIVE OIL

1 TABLESPOON WHITE WINE VINEGAR

2 TABLESPOONS SUGAR

SALT AND PEPPER TO TASTE

KANGAROO

Rub the lemongrass, garlic and pepper into the meat.

Heat the oil in an ovenproof frypan until it is smoking.

Seal each side quickly.

Transfer to a hot oven and roast at 200°C for 10 minutes.

Remove the meat to a plate and leave to rest for 10–15 minutes.

Cut it into very thin slices.

SALAD

Remove and discard the leaves from the bok choy, choy sum and Chinese broccoli.

Cut the stems into fine julienne strips.

Mix with the tatsoi leaves.

Add the grapefruit.

Whisk all the dressing ingredients to combine them and melt the sugar.

Gently fold the dressing into the salad.

Arrange the salad on four plates and top with the warm kangaroo slices.

KANGAROO *with* ASIAN LEAF *and* PINK GRAPEFRUIT SALAD

WHOLE ROASTED GUINEA FOWL STUFFED
with WILD RICE, CELERY *and* APPLE
and SERVED *with* BREAD SAUCE

1 TABLESPOON FRENCH ESCHALOTS,
  FINELY CHOPPED

1 TEASPOON BUTTER

100 GRAMS WILD RICE

1 CUP WHITE WINE

2 CUPS CHICKEN STOCK (SEE PAGE 152)

2 STICKS CELERY, DICED

2 RED APPLES, PEELED, CORED AND DICED

1 TEASPOON BUTTER

2 GUINEA FOWL (NO. 6)

1 TABLESPOON OLIVE OIL

½ TEASPOON SALT

1 TEASPOON FRESH SAGE LEAVES,
  CHOPPED

4 SLICES PROSCIUTTO

Bread Sauce

1 CUP MILK

1 BAYLEAF

¼ TEASPOON NUTMEG

1 CUP FRESH WHITE BREADCRUMBS

1 TEASPOON BUTTER

SALT AND PEPPER TO TASTE

Sauté the eschalots in butter, add the wild rice and stir to coat.

Add the white wine and chicken stock.

Cook until it is soft and the moisture has been absorbed.

Sauté the celery and apple in the butter and add to the rice mixture.

Allow to cool.

Wash and dry the guinea fowl and stuff with the rice mixture.

Truss, then rub the skin with the olive oil, salt and sage.

Lay the prosciutto slices over the breast and roast in the oven at 200°C for 45 minutes.

SAUCE

Bring the milk to a simmer with the bayleaf and nutmeg.

Sprinkle on the breadcrumbs and stir the in butter.

Season to taste.

Stir until thick.

Cut the guinea fowl in half and serve with a little bread sauce.

WHOLE ROASTED GUINEA FOWL STUFFED *with* WILD RICE, CELERY *and* APPLE *and* SERVED *with* BREAD SAUCE

Guinea Fowl Breast Stuffed
with Garlic Chives and Chestnut Mushrooms
and Served with Tart Berry Jam

1 TEASPOON BUTTER

100 GRAMS CHESTNUT MUSHROOMS,
  CUT IN HALF IF LARGE

1 LARGE BUNCH GARLIC CHIVES, TRIMMED
  AND CUT LENGTHWISE INTO 4

SALT AND PEPPER TO TASTE

4 GUINEA FOWL BREASTS,
  APPROXIMATELY 200 GRAMS EACH

1 TABLESPOON OLIVE OIL

1 TEASPOON MELTED BUTTER

Sauce

1 CUP CHICKEN STOCK (SEE PAGE 152)

½ CUP WHITE WINE

1 TABLESPOON SUGAR

1 SPRIG THYME

100 GRAMS CHILLED BUTTER, CUT
  INTO PIECES

Accompaniment

TART BERRY JAM (SEE PAGE 164)

GUINEA FOWL

Melt the butter and sauté the mushrooms for
2 minutes until they are soft.

Add the garlic chives and sauté for 1 minute.

Remove from the heat, season and
allow to cool.

Divide the mixture into four and stuff under
the skin of each guinea fowl breast.

Heat the oil in a frypan over high heat.

Place the breasts in the pan, skin side down.

Lower the heat to medium and cook until the
skin is crispy.

Turn and place the pan in a hot oven at
220°C for 5–7 minutes.

SAUCE

Place the stock, wine, sugar and thyme in
a saucepan and simmer until the liquid is
reduced to half a cup.

Strain. Whisk in the chilled butter pieces.

To serve, pour a little sauce on four warm
plates, place a guinea fowl breast on each.

Accompany with Tart Berry Jam.

Deboned Spatchcock *in* Taro Pastry
with Baby Leeks *and* Lemon-Honey Sauce

4 X NO. 5 SPATCHCOCKS, FULLY BONED

1 CUP CORNFLOUR

Pastry

400 GRAMS TARO, COOKED AND MASHED

1½ CUPS FLOUR

2 EGG WHITES

3 TABLESPOONS BUTTER

1 TABLESPOON VEGETABLE OIL

Leeks

12 BABY LEEKS, WHITE PART ONLY,
   CLEANED WELL

1 LITRE CHICKEN STOCK (SEE PAGE 152)

1 BAYLEAF

¼ TEASPOON BLACK PEPPER,
   COARSELY GROUND

Sauce

½ CUP CHICKEN STOCK (SEE PAGE 152)

½ CUP LEMON JUICE

¼ CUP SUGAR

2 TABLESPOONS WHITE WINE VINEGAR

2 TABLESPOONS CLEAR HONEY

100 GRAMS BUTTER, CHILLED AND CUT
   INTO PIECES

Combine the taro, flour, egg whites, butter and vegetable oil. Knead well, adding more flour if the mixture is too soft.

Cover and leave to rest for 30 minutes.

Divide the pastry evenly into four.

Roll each piece of pastry between two sheets of plastic wrap until it is very thin.

Place a boned spatchcock on each piece, stretching the pastry to cover one side fully.

Gently cover with the cornflour and pat off any excess.

Heat the butter in a large frypan and carefully cook each side until golden brown.

Drain on kitchen paper.

LEEKS

Poach the leeks in the chicken stock with the bayleaf and pepper until they are softened (approximately 15–20 minutes).

Remove with a slotted spoon and keep warm.

SAUCE

Simmer all the ingredients except the butter for 10 minutes.

Remove from the stove and whisk in the butter pieces.

To serve, warm four plates. On each one, place three leeks and a spatchcock.

Pour on a little sauce.

MARINATED RARE ROAST VENISON
with CAJUN SAUCE *and* TART BERRY JAM

2 SPRIGS FRESH THYME

2 SPRIGS FRESH ROSEMARY

1 TEASPOON JUNIPER BERRIES, LIGHTLY
 CRUSHED

2 BAYLEAVES

½ CUP VEGETABLE OIL

1 KG VENISON FILLET

2 TEASPOONS CAJUN PASTE
 (SEE PAGE 169)

1 CUP WATERMARK DEMI-GLAZE
 (SEE PAGE 170)

4 TABLESPOONS TART BERRY JAM
 (SEE PAGE 164)

Remove the leaves from the thyme and rosemary, discard the stalks.

Combine with the juniper berries, bayleaves, oil and venison.

Leave to marinate for at least 2 hours.

Seal the venison quickly, on all sides, in a very hot frypan.

Place in a hot oven at 220°C and roast for 12–15 minutes.

Remove from the oven and leave to rest.

In a small saucepan stir the Cajun Paste over low heat to release the aromas.

Add the demi-glaze and simmer gently for 5 minutes.

Slice the venison thinly.

To serve, pour a little Cajun sauce onto four warm plates and fan the venison on top.

Garnish with Tart Berry Jam.

Notes: Game or beef demi-glaze may be substituted for the Watermark demi-glaze.

Serve with roasted sweet potato and wilted spinach leaves or tatsoi leaves.

MARINATED RARE ROAST VENISON *with* CAJUN SAUCE *and* TART BERRY JAM

BEEF FILLET
with SAUTÉED PUMPKIN, TARO *and* SWEET POTATO
on SHIRAZ GLAZE *with* MUSTARD CREAM

Vegetables

½ CUP OLIVE OIL

1 LARGE SWEET POTATO, PEELED AND CUT
   INTO BATONS

1 TARO, PEELED AND CUT INTO BATONS

½ BUTTERNUT PUMPKIN, PEELED AND
   CUT INTO BATONS

1 TEASPOON BUTTER

1 TEASPOON HONEY

Beef

4 X 220 GRAM EYE FILLET STEAKS, CUT
   FROM THE CENTRE OF A BEEF FILLET

Mustard Cream

1 TABLESPOON DIJON MUSTARD

1 TABLESPOON FRENCH MUSTARD

1 TEASPOON ENGLISH MUSTARD

2 TABLESPOONS DOUBLE CREAM

1 CUP SHIRAZ GLAZE (SEE PAGE 94)

VEGETABLES

Heat the oil in a wok and sauté the sweet
potato and taro for 2 minutes.

Add the pumpkin and continue to sauté until
the batons are firm but cooked.

Remove with a slotted spoon and drain on
paper towels.

Place in a clean frypan, toss in the butter
and honey and place under a hot griller
for 1 minute to glaze.

MUSTARD CREAM

Combine all the mustards and the cream.

Char-grill or pan-fry the beef fillet to the
required taste.

Heat the Shiraz Glaze.

To serve, flood four warm plates with Shiraz
Glaze, divide the vegetable batons into a
stack and top with a beef fillet.

Garnish with Mustard Cream.

BEEF FILLET
with TASMANIAN PEPPER BERRY SAUCE
and TAGLIATELLE *of* CARROT *and* ZUCCHINI

1 TABLESPOON BUTTER

1 KG EYE FILLET STEAKS, CUT FROM THE
   CENTRE OF A BEEF FILLET

Sauce

1 TEASPOON BUTTER

1 TABLESPOON FRENCH ESCHALOTS,
   FINELY CHOPPED

1 TABLESPOON FRESH TARRAGON LEAVES

1 TABLESPOON TASMANIAN PEPPER
   BERRIES, LIGHTLY CRUSHED

2 TABLESPOONS BRANDY

1 CUP BEEF DEMI-GLAZE (SEE PAGE 170)

Vegetables

2 TABLESPOONS OLIVE OIL

1 TEASPOON LEMONGRASS,
   FINELY CHOPPED

2 LARGE CARROTS, SLICED LENGTHWISE,
   VERY THINLY

2 LARGE ZUCCHINI, SLICED LENGTHWISE,
   VERY THINLY

BEEF FILLET

Heat the butter to very hot, then sear the fillet on all sides to seal.

Roast in a hot oven at 220°C for 15–20 minutes.

Remove and rest.

SAUCE

Sauté the eschalots in butter until they are soft.

Add the tarragon and pepper berries.

Add the brandy and stir to release the alcohol.

Add the demi-glaze and simmer gently.

Reduce to three-quarters of a cup.

VEGETABLES

Heat the oil in a wok and sauté the lemongrass for 1 minute.

Add the carrot and zucchini slices and continue to toss until *al dente*.

(Depending on the thickness of the slices, this will not take long.)

To serve, slice the fillet thinly.

Place a little sauce on four warm plates.

Heap the tagliatelle on each plate and fan the beef fillet on top.

Note: Use a potato peeler to make a very fine tagliatelle of carrots and zucchini.

RACK OF LAMB *with* HONEYED ROSELLA FLOWERS, BRIE RAVIOLI *and* WHITE PEPPER SAUCE

1 TABLESPOON VEGETABLE OIL

4 X 4-POINT RACKS OF LAMB, POINTS
  WELL TRIMMED

80 GRAMS BRIE

8 SHEETS GOW GEE PASTRY (SEE PAGE 17)

1 TABLESPOON VEGETABLE OIL

300 ML WHITE PEPPER SAUCE
  (SEE PAGE 158)

4 TABLESPOONS HONEYED ROSELLA
  FLOWERS (SEE PAGE 160)

LAMB

Heat the oil and seal the lamb quickly on all sides.

Wrap the points in foil to avoid burning. Roast in a hot oven at 200°C for 20 minutes.

Remove and leave to rest.

RAVIOLI

Divide the Brie into four equal pieces, then place each piece between two sheets of gow gee pastry.

Seal the edges.

Heat the oil in a frypan and cook the ravioli on both sides until it is golden.

TO ASSEMBLE

Heat the White Pepper Sauce.

Gently warm the rosella flowers.

Cut each rack in half.

Spoon a little sauce onto four warm plates.

Fan the lamb over the sauce, top with a ravioli and garnish with some rosella flowers.

Serve with a simple green leaf salad.

RACK OF LAMB *with* HONEYED ROSELLA FLOWERS, BRIE RAVIOLI *and* WHITE PEPPER SAUCE

HERB-CRUSTED BABY LAMB RUMPS
with ROASTED GARLIC and SAUTÉED POTATOES

1 TABLESPOON OLIVE OIL

4 X 200 GRAMS BABY LAMB RUMPS

2 WHOLE GARLIC, HALVED WIDTHWISE

4 TEASPOONS DIJON MUSTARD

1 BUNCH FLAT-LEAF PARSLEY LEAVES,
CHOPPED

½ BUNCH BASIL LEAVES, CHOPPED

½ BUNCH SAGE LEAVES, CHOPPED

2 TABLESPOONS MINT LEAVES, CHOPPED

1 TEASPOON THYME LEAVES, CHOPPED

GRATED RIND OF 1 LEMON

2 TABLESPOONS OLIVE OIL

1 ONION, CUT INTO JULIENNE STRIPS

1 STICK CELERY, CUT INTO
JULIENNE STRIPS

4 LARGE POTATOES, CUT INTO 2 CM DICE
AND BLANCHED

500 ML LAMB DEMI-GLAZE (SEE PAGE 170)

Heat the oil in a frypan over high heat and seal the lamb on all sides.

Transfer to a hot oven, add the garlic and roast at 200°C for 15 minutes.

Baste with the Dijon mustard and return to the oven for a further 5 minutes.

Remove and leave to rest for 10 minutes.

Combine the chopped herbs and lemon rind.

Roll the lamb in the herb mixture, coating it thoroughly.

Put aside.

POTATOES

Heat the oil in a large frypan and sauté the onion for 2 minutes.

Add the celery and potatoes and sauté them until the potatoes are evenly coloured.

Reduce the lamb demi-glaze to 250 ml.

To serve, pour a little lamb demi-glaze on four warm plates; top with the potatoes.

Slice the lamb thinly and fan it over the top.

Garnish with the roasted garlic.

HERB-CRUSTED BABY LAMB RUMPS *with* ROASTED GARLIC *and* SAUTÉED POTATOES

HONEY-GLAZED VEAL SHANKS

Veal

8 WHOLE VEAL SHANKS

1 ONION, ROUGHLY CHOPPED

2 CARROTS, ROUGHLY CHOPPED

2 STICKS CELERY, ROUGHLY CHOPPED

2 BAYLEAVES

12 FRESH SAGE LEAVES

1 TEASPOON WHOLE PEPPERCORNS

¼ CUP SALT

4 LITRES WATER OR ENOUGH TO
  COVER SHANKS

Glaze

2 CUPS WATERMARK DEMI-GLAZE,
  WARMED (SEE PAGE 170)

4 TEASPOONS HONEY

2 TEASPOONS SUGAR

2 TABLESPOONS FRESH SAGE LEAVES,
  CHOPPED

VEAL

Place the shanks and all the other ingredients for the veal in a large pan or stockpot and cover with water.

Simmer gently for 2 hours.

Remove the shanks. Discard the vegetables.

GLAZE

Place the warm demi-glaze in a roasting pan that is just large enough to hold the shanks.

Add the shanks, brush them with the honey, then sprinkle them with the sugar and sage.

Bake in a hot oven at 220°C for 10 minutes or until the shanks are glazed.

Serve with mounds of creamy mashed potatoes.

Note: This basic veal recipe can be adapted to a variety of sauces.

HONEY-GLAZED VEAL SHANKS

VEAL SHANKS *with* CHUNKY TOMATO *and* RED WINE SAUCE *and* BAKED SWEET POTATOES

8 WHOLE VEAL SHANKS

1 ONION, ROUGHLY CHOPPED

2 CARROTS, ROUGHLY CHOPPED

2 STICKS CELERY, ROUGHLY CHOPPED

2 BAYLEAVES

12 FRESH SAGE LEAVES

1 TEASPOON WHOLE PEPPERCORNS

¼ CUP SALT

4 LITRES WATER OR ENOUGH TO
  COVER SHANKS

Sauce

1 CUP WATERMARK DEMI-GLAZE
  (SEE PAGE 170)

1 CUP CHUNKY TOMATO AND RED WINE
  SAUCE (SEE PAGE 162)

Baked Sweet Potatoes

4 SWEET POTATOES, PEELED

2 TABLESPOONS BUTTER

Place the shanks and all the other ingredients for the veal in a large pan or stockpot and cover with water.

Simmer gently for 2 hours. Remove and discard the vegetables.

Remove the shanks and allow them to cool slightly. Remove the meat from the bone, keeping it together.

Place the veal in an ovenproof dish that is just large enough to hold the eight pieces.

SAUCE

Gently warm the demi-glaze and the Chunky Tomato and Red Wine Sauce.

Pour over the veal and bake in a hot oven at 220°C for 10 minutes.

BAKED SWEET POTATOES

Butter four pieces of foil, then wrap the sweet potatoes.

Bake the potatoes in a hot oven at 200°C for 45 minutes.

To serve, warm four plates and place a potato on each one.

Gently press each potato with a potato masher to make a 'bed' for the veal.

Spoon over the veal and the sauce.

VEAL SHANKS *with* CHUNKY TOMATO *and* RED WINE SAUCE *and* BAKED SWEET POTATOES

VEAL *and* EGGPLANT PARCELS
with COCONUT *and* SWEET CHILLI SAUCE

1 TABLESPOON OLIVE OIL

4 X 200 GRAMS VEAL LOINS

SALT AND PEPPER TO TASTE

1 TABLESPOON OLIVE OIL

1 EGGPLANT, PEELED AND CUT INTO
 JULIENNE STRIPS

1 TEASPOON THAI RED CURRY PASTE

1 TEASPOON TOMATO PASTE

1 TEASPOON SUGAR

4 VIETNAMESE RICE-PAPER WRAPPERS
 (AVAILABLE AT ASIAN GROCERY SHOPS)

HOT WATER

1 TABLESPOON BUTTER, MELTED

2 TABLESPOONS BUTTER

1 TEASPOON FRENCH ESCHALOTS, FINELY
 CHOPPED

½ CUP WATERMARK DEMI-GLAZE
 (SEE PAGE 170)

½ CUP COCONUT CREAM

2 TEASPOONS SWEET CHILLI SAUCE

1 TEASPOON LEMON JUICE

SALT AND PEPPER TO TASTE

Heat the oil in a frypan and seal all sides of the veal loins.

Place the veal in a hot oven and roast at 220°C for 5–7 minutes.

Remove, season to taste and allow to cool.

Sauté the eggplant in hot oil.

Add the curry, tomato paste and sugar.

Cook over low heat until the eggplant is soft but still holds its shape.

Allow to cool.

Using tongs, dip the rice-paper wrappers in hot water for 10 seconds until they are soft.

Place them on a clean tea towel and pat dry.

Divide the eggplant between the four wrappers and top each one with a veal loin.

Wrap up as for spring rolls, encasing the mixture.

Brush the baking tray with half the melted butter; place the parcels on the tray and brush them with the remaining melted butter.

Bake in a hot oven at 220°C for 5 minutes or until the parcels are golden brown and crisp.

SAUCE

Sauté the eschalots in 2 tablespoons of butter until soft.

Add the demi-glaze, coconut cream, chilli sauce and lemon juice.

Simmer gently for 5 minutes. Season to taste.

To serve, flood four warm plates with the sauce and top with a veal parcel.

Note: This dish needs only some steamed rice to accompany it.

VEAL *and* EGGPLANT PARCELS *with* COCONUT *and* SWEET CHILLI SAUCE

RACKS OF VEAL
with FRESH FIGS, PISTACHIO NUTS and VEAL JUS

Figs

50 GRAMS BUTTER

2 TABLESPOONS ONION, FINELY CHOPPED

8 FRESH FIGS, STEMS REMOVED

½ CUP WHITE WINE

1 TABLESPOON FRESH TARRAGON LEAVES,
   CHOPPED

1 TEASPOON SUGAR

½ CUP FRESH WHITE BREADCRUMBS

2 TABLESPOONS FLAT-LEAF PARSLEY,
   CHOPPED

Veal

1 TEASPOON OLIVE OIL

4 X 4-POINT MILK-FED VEAL RACKS

2 CUPS WATERMARK DEMI-GLAZE
   (SEE PAGE 170)

4 TABLESPOONS PISTACHIO NUTS,
   CHOPPED AND LIGHTLY ROASTED

FIGS

Melt the butter in a frypan, add the onion and sauté until it is soft.

Add the figs, white wine, tarragon and sugar.

Cook for 10 minutes, gently mashing the figs.

Remove the pan from the heat and allow to cool slightly.

Add the breadcrumbs and parsley.

VEAL

Heat the oil in a frypan over high heat and quickly seal the veal racks.

Wrap the bones of the veal in foil to avoid burning them.

Transfer the veal to a hot oven and roast it at 220°C for 15 minutes.

Place some fig mixture on top of each rack, dividing it evenly.

Place the racks under a medium-hot griller for 5 minutes or until the crust is crisp.

Place the demi-glaze in a small saucepan and simmer until it is reduced to 150 ml.

To serve, pour a little of the Veal Jus on four warm plates.

Remove the foil from the racks, then arrange them on the plates.

Sprinkle the pistachio nuts over the veal.

Accompany with a tagliatelle of zucchini and carrot (see page 111).

BLUEBERRY BRULÉE

600 ML FRESH CREAM
6 EGG YOLKS
60 GRAMS CASTER SUGAR
1 PUNNET BLUEBERRIES
100 GRAMS CASTER SUGAR

Toffee Garnish
2 CUPS SUGAR
1 CUP WATER

Heat the cream in a saucepan (do not boil).

Whisk the egg yolks and sugar until they are light and fluffy. Slowly stir this into the warmed cream.

Pour the mixture into the top of a double boiler and place it over hot water.

Cook over water that is just simmering, stirring constantly, until the mixture thickens and coats the back of a spoon.

In a small saucepan, gently bring the blueberries and sugar to the boil.

Simmer until most of the moisture has evaporated and a syrup is formed.

Fold the blueberries into the custard mixture and pour it into individual ramekins.

Refrigerate until the custard is set (approximately 2 hours).

TOFFEE GARNISH

Cook the sugar and water in a small saucepan over medium heat until the sugar dissolves.

Increase the heat and cook, without stirring, until the mixture turns a golden toffee colour.

Remove and quickly pour the toffee onto a marble slab or a baking tray lined with foil. (This mixture is extremely hot.) When it has cooled and set, break off pieces of toffee to fit the top of the ramekins.

Use a red hot brulée iron or place under a hot griller to melt the toffee.

VARIATION

Sprinkle each custard with caster sugar, completely covering the custard.

Place the moulds in a baking tray and surround with ice, making sure the ice comes at least two-thirds of the way up the moulds.

Place under a very hot griller until the sugar is caramelised. (It's important to do this very quickly. If the inside custard becomes too hot, it will scramble and become grainy.)

Serve with a side dish of fresh blueberries.

BLUEBERRY BRULÉE

APRICOT SAUTERNE JELLY
and MANGO BAVAROIS

Jelly

300 ML SAUTERNE OR DESSERT WINE

200 ML APRICOT JUICE

1 STICK OF CINNAMON

1 TEASPOON GELATINE

Bavarois

250 ML MANGO PUREÉ

1 TEASPOON GELATINE

1 NIP VODKA (OPTIONAL)

500 ML CREAM

75 GRAMS SUGAR

JELLY

Gently heat the wine and apricot juice with the cinnamon stick.

At simmering point, remove from the heat and dissolve the gelatine in the hot liquid.

Strain and allow to cool.

Pour the jelly into individual moulds, filling them to halfway.

Leave to set.

BAVAROIS

Heat the mango pureé to simmering point, then remove it from the heat and dissolve the gelatine in the pureé.

Add a nip of vodka, if desired, and allow the mango mousse to cool.

Whisk the cream and sugar until the mixture forms soft peaks, then fold it into the cool mango mousse.

Pour the Bavarois onto the firm jelly and leave it to set for 2–3 hours (it can be covered and left overnight in the refrigerator).

To serve, dip the mould quickly into hot water and turn it out onto individual plates.

Garnish with fresh fruit, such as strawberries, mango slices, raspberries and blueberries.

CARAMELISED APPLES
with BRANDY SABAYON *and* SHORTBREAD

Apples
200 GRAMS BROWN SUGAR

125 GRAMS UNSALTED BUTTER

4 GREEN APPLES, PEELED AND CORED

Sabayon
4 EGG YOLKS

100 GRAMS SUGAR

50 ML BRANDY

Shortbread
2 CUPS PLAIN FLOUR, SIFTED

2 TABLESPOONS GROUND RICE
   FLOUR, SIFTED

¼ CUP ICING SUGAR, SIFTED

175 GRAMS UNSALTED BUTTER,
   CUT INTO PIECES

APPLES

Heat the brown sugar and butter in a pan large enough to hold the apples in one layer.

Cook until the sugar is melted.

Add the apples and cook over low heat for 5 minutes, turning constantly.

SABAYON

Bring the water in a double boiler just to a simmer over medium heat. In the top of the double boiler, whisk together the egg yolks, sugar and brandy.

Whisk constantly until the mixture is light and fluffy and has quadrupled in volume. Do not overheat or the egg yolks will scramble.

Remove from the heat and continue to whisk for 3–4 minutes (this will help to stop the mixture from collapsing).

SHORTBREAD

Place the sifted flours and icing sugar in a bowl and rub in the butter.

Knead the mixture quickly until it is smooth.

Roll the dough between two sheets of plastic wrap until it is 1 cm thick.

Cut into the desired shapes, such as stars, and place them on an ungreased baking tray.

Bake in a warm oven at 180°C until the biscuits are a light golden brown (approximately 15–20 minutes).

To serve, place an apple on four warm dessert plates, pour over a little sabayon and accompany with the shortbreads on the side.

Note: This shortbread recipe is quite generous. Any leftovers will keep in an airtight container.

BANANA, PASSIONFRUIT *and* RICOTTA BASKETS

Baskets

4 SHEETS FILO PASTRY, CUT INTO
   QUARTERS

2 TABLESPOONS MELTED BUTTER

Filling

200 GRAMS FRESH RICOTTA CHEESE

2 BANANAS, PEELED AND DICED

4 PASSIONFRUITS, CUT IN HALF AND
   PULP REMOVED

50 ML GALLIANO

CASTER SUGAR TO TASTE

Garnish

2 PASSIONFRUIT, CUT IN HALF

Place four dariole moulds upside down on a lightly buttered baking tray.

Brush each quartered filo sheet with melted butter and, with the buttered side down, lay them over a dariole mould.

Allow the excess pastry to lay on the baking tray in order to create a basket effect.

Repeat this process, using a total of four sheets per mould. Bake at 180°C until golden brown (approximately 10 minutes).

Remove the baking tray from the oven and allow the pastry to cool.

Carefully turn the pastry and moulds upright.

Remove the moulds.

FILLING

Gently mix all the ingredients.

Add the sugar last of all and adjust to taste.

To serve, spoon the filling into the pastry baskets and serve immediately on four dessert plates, garnished with the passionfruit halves.

BANANA, PASSIONFRUIT *and* RICOTTA BASKETS

MARINATED SUMMER FRUITS

100 ML FRESH ORANGE JUICE

100 ML FRESH APPLE JUICE

100 ML FRESH PINEAPPLE JUICE

2 CLOVES

½ CINNAMON STICK

50 ML COINTREAU

½ SMALL HONEYDEW MELON, PEELED AND
  CUT INTO CHUNKS

½ SMALL ROCKMELON, PEELED AND CUT
  INTO CHUNKS

½ SMALL PINEAPPLE, PEELED AND CUT
  INTO CHUNKS

1 MANGO, PEELED AND SLICED

2 PEACHES, STONED AND SLICED

STRAWBERRIES

BLACKBERRIES

RASPBERRIES

BLUEBERRIES

Place the juices, cloves and cinnamon in a small saucepan.

Gently bring this mixture to the boil.

Allow it to cool, then pour it into a glass or ceramic bowl.

Add the Cointreau.

Add the two types of melon, the pineapple, mango and peaches.

Cover and leave to marinate overnight in the refrigerator.

Just before serving, add the berries.

Serve with shortbread stars (see page 127).

Note: Any fruits can be used, there is no need to restrict yourself.

If you are using berries, add them just before serving or the marinade will be coloured and the berries will break up.

MARINATED SUMMER FRUITS

SORBETS *in a* ROSEWATER ICE BASKET

Lemon

450 GRAMS CASTER SUGAR

450 ML STILL MINERAL WATER

2 EGG WHITES

JUICE OF 1 LEMON

Lime

450 GRAMS CASTER SUGAR

450 ML STILL MINERAL WATER

2 EGG WHITES

JUICE OF 4 LIMES

Passionfruit

450 GRAMS CASTER SUGAR

450 ML STILL MINERAL WATER

4 EGG WHITES

PULP OF 6 PASSIONFRUIT

Rosewater Basket

250 ML STILL MINERAL WATER

15 ML ROSEWATER

1 DROP RED FOOD COLOURING

8 BRIOCHE MOULDS

SORBETS

Use the following method for each flavour.

Boil the sugar and water to the soft ball stage (116–118°C on a sugar thermometer).

In an electric mixer, whisk the egg whites until they are stiff.

Gradually add the boiled sugar syrup to the egg whites, whisking all the time until the mixture is cool.

Fold the fruit juice or pulp through the mixture.

Churn it in an ice-cream machine, following the manufacturer's instructions.

ROSEWATER BASKET

Combine the water, rosewater and colouring.

Pour 0.5 cm into each of four brioche moulds.

Freeze.

Over a tray or sink, pour more rosewater liquid onto the frozen rosewater until each mould is two-thirds full.

Place another brioche mould on top of the rosewater and push down lightly.

Freeze.

Remove the moulds from the freezer; quickly dip the base of each one into hot water.

Remove the brioche moulds and fill the ice baskets with the sorbets.

Serve immediately.

Note: It is best to use still mineral water to avoid the chlorine taste detectable in the tap water in some areas of Australia.

SORBETS *in a* ROSEWATER ICE BASKET

STEAMED FIG *and* GINGER PUDDING *with*
BUTTERSCOTCH SAUCE *and* FIG *and* GINGER COMPOTE

Pudding

60 GRAMS BUTTER
80 GRAMS CASTER SUGAR
2 EGG YOLKS
170 GRAMS SELF-RAISING FLOUR
½ TEASPOON BICARBONATE OF SODA
½ TEASPOON MIXED SPICE
1 TEASPOON GROUND GINGER
80 ML MILK
A FEW DROPS OF VANILLA ESSENCE
85 GRAMS DRIED FIGS, ROUGHLY CHOPPED
2 EGG WHITES
MELTED BUTTER

Butterscotch Sauce

200 GRAMS CASTER SUGAR
300 ML FRESH CREAM
1 TABLESPOON UNSALTED BUTTER

Fig and Ginger Compote

250 GRAMS DRIED FIGS, CUT INTO
    QUARTERS
2 CM PIECE FRESH GINGER, PEELED AND
    CUT INTO FINE JULIENNE STRIPS
½ CUP SAUTERNE
½ CUP HONEY

PUDDING

Cream the butter and sugar until it is light and fluffy.

Add the egg yolks one by one, beating the mixture well after each addition.

Add the flour, soda, mixed spice and ground ginger, then the milk and vanilla and mix well.

Fold in the dried figs.

Whip the egg whites until they are stiff and gently fold them into the flour mixture.

Grease a 1 litre pudding bowl with the melted butter, pour in the mixture and cover it tightly with foil.

Place in a large saucepan.

Pour in enough simmering water to come two-thirds of the way up the pudding bowl.

Cover the saucepan and steam the pudding for 2 hours on medium heat.

Check the water level throughout, topping up as necessary.

BUTTERSCOTCH SAUCE

In a small saucepan, cook the sugar over medium heat until it caramelises.

As soon as it turns a light brown colour, pour the sugar carefully into the cream.

Add the butter and mix well.

Cook for a further 5 minutes.

COMPOTE

Place all the ingredients in a small saucepan and simmer the compote gently until the figs are soft (approximately 15 minutes).

TO ASSEMBLE

Turn the pudding onto a serving plate.

Spoon a little compote on the top.

Serve with the butterscotch sauce and some extra compote on the side.

STEAMED FIG *and* GINGER PUDDING *with* BUTTERSCOTCH SAUCE *and* FIG *and* GINGER COMPOTE

LUSCIOUS LEMON CURD TART

Pastry

115 GRAMS UNSALTED BUTTER

50 GRAMS CASTER SUGAR

1 EGG

250 GRAMS PLAIN FLOUR

Filling

250 ML LEMON JUICE

150 GRAMS UNSALTED BUTTER

250 GRAMS CASTER SUGAR

250 ML WHOLE EGGS

3 GELATINE LEAVES, SOFTENED IN A
   LITTLE COLD WATER

PASTRY

Cream the butter and sugar, add the egg, then sift in the flour and mix it thoroughly.

Wrap the dough in plastic wrap and leave it to rest for 30 minutes in the refrigerator.

Remove. Roll out the dough to a thickness of 5 mm, then line a 25 cm flan tin.

Place it in a hot oven. Blind bake the pastry at 160°C for 30 minutes or until it is golden.

Remove the pastry from the oven and allow it to cool in the tin.

FILLING

Heat the lemon juice and butter until they are boiling.

Whisk the sugar and eggs until they are creamy.

Slowly pour the hot juice into the egg mixture, stirring constantly.

Transfer the mixture to the top of a double boiler and place it over simmering water.

Cook, stirring, until the mixture thoroughly coats the back of a spoon.

Remove it from the heat.

Squeeze the water from the soaked gelatine leaves, then stir the gelatine into the lemon mixture.

Allow the mixture to cool slightly, then pour it into the baked flan case.

Refrigerate until the tart is firm.

Serve with double cream and strawberries marinated in Cointreau.

Note: Three gelatine leaves are equal to 1½ teaspoons powdered gelatine.

Gelatine leaves give a smoother, superior result.

LUSCIOUS LEMON CURD TART

BAKED DOUBLE-CHOCOLATE CAKE
with LICORICE SYRUP

Double-Chocolate Cake

BUTTER AND FLOUR TO LINE CAKE TIN
500 GRAMS DARK CHOCOLATE
350 GRAMS UNSALTED BUTTER
12 EGGS
280 GRAMS CASTER SUGAR
60 GRAMS SELF-RAISING FLOUR

Licorice Syrup

500 ML WATER
20 GRAMS LIQUORICE ROOT
75 GRAMS SUGAR
25 GRAMS DARK CHOCOLATE

DOUBLE-CHOCOLATE CAKE

Brush a 30 cm springform cake tin with a little melted butter, then dust it lightly with flour, making sure that all the sides are coated.

Shake out any excess flour.

Melt the chocolate and butter in the top of a double boiler over hot water.

Allow this to cool slightly.

Whisk the eggs and sugar until they are very light and fluffy.

Fold in the flour.

Gently fold in the melted chocolate.

Pour the mixture into the prepared cake tin and bake at 160°C for 1 hour.

Remove the cake from the oven and allow it to cool in the tin.

LICORICE SYRUP

Place all the ingredients into a saucepan and slowly bring them to the boil.

Simmer on low heat until the mixture is reduced by half (approximately 1 hour).

Strain and leave to cool, preferably overnight.

To serve, flood plates with the syrup, then place a wedge of cake on top.

Add a dollop of double cream for sheer decadence.

BAKED DOUBLE-CHOCOLATE CAKE *with* LICORICE SYRUP

ORANGE *and* POPPY SEED TORTE
with a COINTREAU GLAZE

Torte

2 LARGE ORANGES

6 EGGS

1 CUP CASTER SUGAR

1½ CUPS GROUND ALMOND MEAL

½ CUP POPPY SEEDS

1 TEASPOON BAKING POWER

BUTTER AND FLOUR TO LINE TIN

Cointreau Glaze

JUICE OF 2 ORANGES

½ TEASPOON ARROWROOT

2 ORANGES PEELED AND SEGMENTED
(PIPS REMOVED)

125 ML COINTREAU

PEEL FROM 2 ORANGES, CUT INTO
JULIENNE STRIPS AND BLANCHED
(AS PER DUCK AND ORANGE SAUCE
RECIPE PAGE 156)

TORTE

Place the oranges, unpeeled, in a pan, cover them with water and boil for 2 hours, adding more water if necessary.

Drain and allow to cool, remove the pips, then pulp in a food processor.

Beat the eggs and sugar to combine, then stir in the ground almonds and poppy seeds.

Add the pulped oranges.

Add the baking powder.

Grease and flour a loose-bottomed cake tin.

Pour in the mixture and bake it at 180°C for approximately 1 hour.

Allow the torte to cool in the tin.

GLAZE

Warm the orange juice, then add the arrowroot to thicken it slightly.

Allow to cool.

Add the segmented oranges and Cointreau.

To serve, pour a little glaze on each plate. Add a piece of the torte, then pour over a little more of the glaze.

Decorate with the julienne of peel.

ORANGE *and* POPPY SEED TORTE *with a* COINTREAU GLAZE

WHITE CHOCOLATE *and* MASCARPONE BAVAROIS

230 ML CREAM

450 GRAMS WHITE CHOCOLATE

2 GELATINE LEAVES, SOFTENED IN A LITTLE
   COLD WATER

375 ML CREAM, SOFT WHIPPED

375 GRAMS MASCARPONE

JUICE OF ½ LEMON

2 TABLESPOONS KIRSCH

Heat the cream and chocolate in a saucepan over low heat, stirring constantly, until the chocolate has melted.

Squeeze the water from the soaked gelatine leaves. Add the gelatine to the chocolate mix.

Stir to dissolve.

Allow to cool slightly.

Fold together half of the soft whipped cream and all of the mascarpone.

Fold this into the chocolate mixture.

Add the lemon juice and Kirsch.

Fold in the remaining cream and pour the bavarois into individual moulds.

Cover and leave to chill for 3–4 hours or overnight. Serve with fresh fruits or Marinated Summer Fruits (see page 130).

Notes: The bavarois in our photo was made in a square cake tin and cut into squares to serve.

Dariole or individual soufflé moulds are also ideal.

WHITE CHOCOLATE *and* MASCARPONE BAVAROIS

WATERMARK SOUFFLÉ

200 ML MILK

1 VANILLA BEAN

1 EGG

2 EGG YOLKS

50 GRAMS CASTER SUGAR

25 GRAMS PLAIN FLOUR, SIFTED

8 EGG WHITES

4 TABLESPOONS CASTER SUGAR

Heat the milk and vanilla bean to simmering.

Beat the egg, egg yolks and sugar.

Add the flour and mix until it is smooth.

Remove the vanilla bean from the milk and gradually pour the warm milk over the flour mixture, whisking to avoid lumps.

Pour the mixture into a clean saucepan and cook it over medium heat, whisking, until the consistency is smooth and the flour is cooked out (do not boil).

Allow to cool.

Whisk the egg whites and sugar until firm.

Gently blend one-third of the egg whites into the cooled milk and flour mixture.

Gently fold the remaining two-thirds of the egg white into the mixture.

Spoon into four greased soufflé moulds. Cook in a hot oven at 190°C for 20–25 minutes.

Serve immediately.

VARIATIONS

LIQUEUR SOUFFLÉ

Substitute 100 ml Grand Marnier, Cointreau or Kirsch for half the milk.

CHOCOLATE

Add 60 grams of good quality grated chocolate to the hot milk.

ALMOND OR HAZELNUT

Add 120 grams of ground nuts to the milk.

COFFEE

Substitute 60 ml of strong black coffee for 60 ml of the milk.

CHERRIES

Add 200 grams of pitted cherries to the cooled milk and flour mixture.

WATERMARK SOUFFLÉ

CHICKEN *and* VEGETABLE BROTH
with CHICKEN DUMPLINGS

Dumplings

500 GRAMS MINCED, RAW CHICKEN MEAT,
  PREFERABLY FROM THE BREAST

¼ ONION, FINELY CHOPPED

½ CELERY STICK, FINELY CHOPPED

2 DROPS TABASCO SAUCE

PINCH SALT

2 PINCHES SUGAR

2 EGG WHITES

SIMMERING WATER

Vegetables

1 SMALL DAIKON (JAPANESE WHITE
  RADISH), PEELED AND CUT INTO FINE
  JULIENNE STRIPS

1 LEEK, WHITE PART ONLY, WASHED WELL
  AND CUT INTO FINE JULIENNE STRIPS

1 SMALL RED CAPSICUM, PEELED AND CUT
  INTO FINE JULIENNE STRIPS

1 TEASPOON OLIVE OIL

½ BUNCH TATSOI LEAVES, WASHED

1 LITRE CHICKEN STOCK (SEE PAGE 152)

DUMPLINGS

Place the chicken, onion, celery, Tabasco sauce, salt and sugar in a food processor or blender and pulse for a few seconds.

Lightly whisk the egg whites, then fold them through the chicken mixture.

Form the mixture into small balls and poach them in simmering water for 5 minutes.

Remove with a slotted spoon.

VEGETABLES

Sauté the julienne of daikon, leek and capsicum in hot olive oil for 3 minutes or until the vegetable are beginning to soften.

Remove from the pan.

TO ASSEMBLE

Heat the chicken stock until it is simmering.

Add the dumplings, vegetables and tatsoi leaves.

Remove from the heat and serve immediately in four warm soup dishes.

Note: The chicken dumplings can be poached in the stock, but this will somewhat cloud the appearance of the dish.

LIGHT CURRIED SHELLFISH SOUP

Soup
2 TABLESPOONS OLIVE OIL
1 KG PRAWN HEADS AND SMALL CRABS,
  BROKEN INTO SMALL PIECES
½ CUP FRENCH ESCHALOTS, PEELED
  AND ROUGHLY CHOPPED
2 CELERY STICKS, WASHED AND ROUGHLY
  CHOPPED
1 ONION, PEELED AND ROUGHLY CHOPPED
1 LEEK, WASHED WELL AND ROUGHLY
  CHOPPED
2 CARROTS, PEELED AND ROUGHLY
  CHOPPED
2 TABLESPOONS CURRY POWDER
½ CUP TOMATO PASTE
100 ML BRANDY
500 ML WHITE WINE
2 LITRES WATER
½ LITRE CREAM
1 SPRIG FRESH THYME
1 BAYLEAF
5 WHOLE PEPPERCORNS
SALT AND WHITE PEPPER

Garnish
20 PRAWNS
20 SCALLOPS
100 GRAMS COOKED CRABMEAT

Heat the olive oil in a pan.

Sauté the shellfish, eschalots, celery, onion, leek and carrots until they are golden in colour and softened.

Add the curry powder and stir rapidly to release the flavours.

Add the tomato paste and stir in briskly, then pour in the brandy and white wine.

Cook over high heat, stirring constantly to release the alcohol.

Add the water and simmer for 20 minutes.

Strain and place in a clean stockpot.

Add the cream, thyme, bayleaf and peppercorns.

Simmer, skimming as necessary, and reduce to 1 litre (approximately 1½ hours).

Strain; season to taste.

TO ASSEMBLE

Poach the prawns and scallops in the simmering curry soup until they are just cooked (approximately 2 minutes).

Remove and distribute between four soup dishes.

Divide the crabmeat into the dishes, then pour over the hot curry soup.

Serve immediately.

Note: Any fish or seafood can be substituted for the garnish.

HOT *and* SOUR CRAB SOUP

Soup

1 LITRE FISH STOCK (SEE PAGE 153)

1 TABLESPOON TOMATO PASTE

1 LITRE TOMATO JUICE

250 ML WHITE WINE

3 TABLESPOONS WHITE WINE VINEGAR

100 GRAMS BROWN SUGAR

2 SMALL FRESH RED CHILLIES, SEEDED AND
CHOPPED

2 STEMS LEMONGRASS, THINLY SLICED

3 STEMS CORIANDER

1/2 LEMON (OR 1 LIME CUT IN HALF)

Garnish

1 LEEK, CUT INTO THIN JULIENNE STRIPS

1 CARROT, PEELED AND CUT INTO THIN
JULIENNE STRIPS

2 TABLESPOONS CORIANDER LEAVES,
ROUGHLY CHOPPED

200 GRAMS COOKED CRABMEAT

Place all the soup ingredients in a stockpot and simmer them for approximately 1½ hours or until they have reduced to 1 litre.

Strain.

Adjust the sugar and vinegar to taste.

Poach the julienne of leek and carrot in the simmering soup base for 3 minutes.

Divide the coriander and crabmeat into four soup dishes.

Pour over the hot soup. Serve immediately.

Note: For those who like their soup particularly hot, add to the garnish some finely chopped red chilli and spring onion.

SAKE SHARK SOUP

100 GRAMS SHARK'S FIN IN THE PIECE
(PREFERABLY A THICK PIECE), COVERED
IN COLD WATER AND LEFT TO SOAK FOR
1 HOUR, THEN DRAINED

1 LITRE CHICKEN STOCK (SEE PAGE 152)

200 ML SAKE

2 SLICES PEELED GINGER

SALT AND WHITE PEPPER

Bring the chicken stock, sake and ginger to a simmer, then cook the mixture for 10 minutes to release the alcohol.

Remove the ginger and add the drained shark's fin.

Simmer until the shark's fin is soft (approximately 5 minutes). The shark's fin will separate into the stock.

Season to taste and serve.

Notes: The thicker pieces of shark's fin are of better quality than the skinny end pieces.

It is important to cook out the alcohol in the sake as the flavour becomes sweeter as the alcohol dissipates.

MUSHROOM *and* EGG WHITE SOUP

1 TABLESPOON OLIVE OIL

50 GRAMS WHITE BUTTON MUSHROOMS,
SLICED

50 GRAMS OYSTER MUSHROOMS, SLICED

50 GRAMS CHESTNUT MUSHROOMS, SLICED

50 GRAMS BROWN MUSHROOMS, SLICED

100 ML WHITE WINE

1 LITRE CHICKEN STOCK (SEE PAGE 152)

100 ML OYSTER SAUCE

1 LEMON LEAF (OR LIME LEAF)

3 EGG WHITES

PINCH SUGAR

SALT AND WHITE PEPPER TO TASTE

Heat the oil, then sauté all the mushrooms until they are soft.

Add the white wine and cook the mixture to release the alcohol (approximately 2 minutes).

Add the stock, oyster sauce and lemon leaf. Simmer for 15 minutes.

Whisk the egg whites lightly to combine. Slowly pour the egg whites into the simmering stock, moving the stock with a whisk in a steady motion to create threads of egg white.

Remove immediately from the heat.

Add a pinch of sugar and season if necessary.

Serve in soup dishes, distributing the mushrooms evenly.

Note: Experiment with any combination of mushrooms to equal 200 grams.

WATERMARK BOUILLABAISSE

1 LITRE FISH STOCK (SEE PAGE 153)

2 TABLESPOONS OLIVE OIL

4 WHOLE BLUE SWIMMER CRABS, CLEANED AND QUARTERED

1 FRENCH ESCHALOT, PEELED AND FINELY CHOPPED

1 FRESH CHILLI, SEEDED AND FINELY SLICED

20 PIPIS, SOAKED IN COLD WATER FOR 1 HOUR, THEN DRAINED

4 YABBIES

4–8 SCAMPI

4–8 GREEN PRAWNS, SHELLED AND DEVEINED

12–16 SEA SCALLOPS

200–300 GRAMS FIRM FLESHED FISH, CUT INTO 2 CM PIECES (BLUE-EYE COD, ATLANTIC SALMON, OCEAN TROUT ARE ALL SUITABLE TYPES OF FISH)

100 ML WHITE WINE

1 TABLESPOON PERNOD

1 BAYLEAF

1 LEEK, CUT INTO VERY FINE JULIENNE STRIPS

1 CELERY STICK, CUT INTO VERY FINE JULIENNE STRIPS

1 LARGE TOMATO, PEELED, SEEDED AND CHOPPED INTO 2 CM DICE

2 TABLESPOONS CORIANDER LEAVES, ROUGHLY CHOPPED

SALT AND WHITE PEPPER TO TASTE

Heat the fish stock until it is simmering.

Meanwhile, heat the olive oil, then sauté the crabs, eschalot and chilli for 5 minutes.

Add the pipis and the remainder of the seafood and fish, then sauté for 1 minute.

Add the white wine, Pernod and bayleaf. Cook quickly to release the alcohol.

Add the julienne of leek and celery and the hot stock. Simmer for 1 minute.

Remove from the heat, add the tomato and coriander, then season.

Remove the bayleaf and serve immediately, distributing the seafood evenly among the soup plates.

Notes: Adapt the seafood and fish according to what is available fresh at the markets.

This substantial main course dish needs little other than a good bread to soak up the juices.

CHICKEN STOCK

2 KG CHICKEN BONES

HOT WATER

1 ONION, ROUGHLY CHOPPED

1 LEEK, WASHED WELL AND
  ROUGHLY CHOPPED

2 CELERY STICKS, WASHED AND
  ROUGHLY CHOPPED

4–5 WHITE MUSHROOMS,
  ROUGHLY CHOPPED

1 BAYLEAF

6 WHOLE PEPPERCORNS

500 ML WHITE WINE

3 LITRES WATER

SALT TO TASTE

Wash the bones in the hot water.

Drain, then place the chicken bones and all the other ingredients in a stockpot.

Simmer, skimming occasionally, until the liquid reduces to 1 litre (approximately 2 hours).

Strain, season, allow to cool, then refrigerate. Skim off any fat.

Use for soups and sauces.

Note: Washing the chicken bones first in hot water cooks any blood and gives a clearer stock.

FISH STOCK

1 KG FISH BONES, BODIES ONLY (SEE NOTE)

HOT WATER

1 ONION, CHOPPED

1 LEEK, WASHED WELL AND ROUGHLY
    CHOPPED

1 CELERY STICK, WASHED AND ROUGHLY
    CHOPPED

1 FRENCH ESCHALOT, PEELED AND
    ROUGHLY CHOPPED

3–4 WHITE MUSHROOMS, ROUGHLY
    CHOPPED

1 BAYLEAF

2 SPRIGS PARSLEY ON THE STALK, WASHED

1 SPRIG FRESH THYME, WASHED

3 SLICES OF LEMON

250 ML WHITE WINE

1 LITRE WATER

SALT TO TASTE

Wash the fish bones well in the hot water.

Drain, then place the bones and all the other ingredients in a stockpot.

Heat until simmering, then cook for 20 minutes, skimming occasionally.

Strain. Return the strained stock to a clean pan and cook until it is reduced to 500 ml.

Season, allow to cool, then refrigerate.

Remove any fat before using.

Notes: Washing the fish bones first in hot water removes any blood and makes a clearer stock.

Using fish body bones rather than heads gives a whiter and less oily stock.

SEAFOOD STOCK VARIATION

Substitute the equivalent amount of prawn heads and shells and/or small crabs broken into pieces for the fish bones.

Sauté in a little hot oil to just colour.

Add the vegetables and liquid, then proceed as for the fish stock recipe.

GARLIC *and* GINGER STOCK

20 GRAMS GARLIC, FINELY GRATED

20 GRAMS GINGER, FINELY GRATED

1 TEASPOON OLIVE OIL

100 ML GINGER WINE

50 ML WHITE WINE VINEGAR

500 ML WATER

250 GRAMS WHITE SUGAR

PINCH OF SALT

Sauté the garlic and ginger in the oil over low heat until it is softened (do not allow it to burn).

Add the ginger wine and wine vinegar, then turn up the heat.

Cook for 1 minute to release the alcohol, then add the water, sugar and salt.

Simmer slowly and reduce to approximately 250 ml. (It is important to simmer slowly to attain a richness of flavour. Reduce the sauce further if more sweetness is desired.)

VARIATIONS

To develop this into a soup base, substitute 500 ml chicken or fish stock for the water.

For a ginger wine substitute, mix 500 grams peeled and chopped ginger and 750 ml sweet wine or medium sweet sherry. Store in a jar in the refrigerator and leave for one week before using in order to infuse the flavours. Keeps indefinitely.

DUCK STOCK

BONES FROM A WHOLE DUCK

1 TABLESPOON OLIVE OIL

1 ONION, CHOPPED

1 LEEK, WASHED WELL AND CHOPPED

2 CELERY STICKS, WASHED AND CHOPPED

1 CARROT, PEELED AND CHOPPED

2 TABLESPOONS TOMATO PASTE

500 ML RED WINE

1 SPRIG OF FRESH TARRAGON

3 LITRES WATER

SALT AND WHITE PEPPER TO TASTE

Chop the duck bones into small pieces. Sauté them in hot oil until they are brown and aromatic.

Add the onion, leek, celery and carrot and continue to sauté until they are soft and golden in colour. Add the tomato paste and stir well.

Add the red wine and tarragon. Cook over high heat to release the alcohol.

Add the water. Bring the mixture to the boil, then turn down the heat and simmer slowly, skimming as necessary, until the liquid is reduced to around 500 ml when strained (approximately 2 hours). Season to taste.

Note: Leftover bones from a roast duck may be substituted.

DUCK *and* ORANGE SAUCE

1 LITRE ORANGE JUICE

500 ML DUCK STOCK (SEE PAGE 155)

10 WHOLE PEPPERCORNS

1 WHOLE ORANGE, PEELED, SEGMENTED
  AND PIPS REMOVED

PEEL FROM ORANGE CUT INTO JULIENNE
  STRIPS

3 CUPS WATER

1 CUP WHITE SUGAR

Heat the orange juice until it reduces to 500 ml. Add the duck stock and peppercorns, then reduce again to 500 ml. Strain.

To segment the orange, cut away the peel in long strips, then remove all the white pith encasing the orange. With a sharp knife, cut out each orange segment, leaving behind the thin membrane.

To prepare a julienne of orange peel, use a vegetable peeler to remove only the orange part of the rind (the white pith next to the flesh is bitter and must be discarded).

Cut the peel into very thin strips. Blanch the strips in hot water for 2 minutes, then drain and refresh in cold water.

Place the julienne, water and sugar in a pan. Bring to the boil, simmer for 5 minutes, then drain.

Just before serving, add the orange segments and julienne peel to the sauce to warm through.

SAKE *and* BASIL SAUCE

1 TABLESPOON OLIVE OIL

2 FRENCH ESCHALOTS, FINELY DICED

250 ML SAKE

50 ML WHITE WINE VINEGAR

500 ML WATER

100 GRAMS WHITE SUGAR

4 BASIL STEMS, LEAVES REMOVED

4 TABLESPOONS BASIL LEAVES, FINELY
  CHOPPED

SALT AND WHITE PEPPER TO TASTE

Heat the olive oil, then sauté the eschalots until they are soft.

Add the sake and white wine vinegar, then cook for 2 minutes over high heat.

Add the water, sugar and basil stems.

Simmer and reduce by half (to approximately 250 ml). Remove the basil stems.

Add the basil leaves. Remove from the heat and season to taste.

Serve with fish, scallops or salmon.

Notes: It is important to remove the sauce from the heat as soon as the basil leaves are added in order to retain the colour and freshness of the basil. The sauce can be prepared to the reduction stage, cooled, then reheated later. Add the basil to the hot sauce just before serving.

GINGER *and* WHITE WINE SAUCE

1 TABLESPOON OLIVE OIL

100 GRAMS GINGER, PEELED AND GRATED

1 TABLESPOON FRESH TARRAGON LEAVES,
  CHOPPED

500 ML WHITE WINE

250 ML WATER

2 TABLESPOONS WHITE SUGAR

SALT AND WHITE PEPPER TO TASTE

Heat the olive oil, then sauté the ginger and tarragon for approximately 2 minutes.

Add the white wine and cook over high heat to release the alcohol.

Add the water and sugar, then simmer until reduced by two-thirds (to approximately 250 ml).

Serve with seafood.

VARIATION

For a stronger flavoured sauce to accompany duck or beef, substitute 250 ml duck or beef stock for the water.

LIGHT CURRY SAUCE

1 TABLESPOON OLIVE OIL

½ LARGE ONION, FINELY SLICED

1 PIECE OF GINGER (ABOUT 3 CM) SLICED

3 TABLESPOONS CURRY POWDER

2 TABLESPOONS TOMATO PASTE

100 ML WHITE WINE

1 BAYLEAF

750 ML WATER

250 ML COCONUT CREAM

1 CINNAMON STICK, BROKEN IN HALF

SALT AND WHITE PEPPER TO TASTE

Heat the olive oil, then sauté the onion and ginger until they are soft.

Add the curry powder and cook it quickly to release the flavours. Add the tomato paste, white wine and bayleaf.

Cook over high heat to release the alcohol.

Add the water, coconut cream and cinnamon stick.

Simmer until the liquid reduces by three-quarters (to approximately 300 ml). Strain and season.

Serve with vegetables, chicken or fish.

Note: For a stronger flavoured sauce, replace the water with chicken or fish stock, as appropriate.

BLACK PEPPER SAUCE

1 ONION, MINCED OR VERY FINELY DICED

1 TABLESPOON LEMONGRASS, FINELY SLICED

1 TABLESPOON OLIVE OIL

2 TABLESPOONS CRUSHED BLACK
   PEPPERCORNS

1 TABLESPOON TOMATO PASTE

50 ML BRANDY

1 TABLESPOON FRESH TARRAGON LEAVES

1 BAYLEAF

500 ML WATERMARK DEMI-GLAZE
   (SEE PAGE 170)

Sauté the onion and lemongrass in the olive oil over slow heat until they are soft.

Add the pepper and stir for 1 minute.

Add the tomato paste and brandy, then stir.

Add the tarragon, bayleaf and demi-glaze.

Simmer until the liquid reduces by half (to approximately 250 ml).

Remove the bayleaf and serve with beef or veal.

WHITE PEPPER SAUCE

1 TABLESPOON OLIVE OIL

½ ONION, MINCED OR FINELY DICED

2 TABLESPOONS WHITE PEPPERCORNS,
   FINELY CRUSHED

250 ML WHITE WINE

1 BAYLEAF

500 ML CHICKEN STOCK (SEE PAGE 152)

250 ML CREAM

Heat the olive oil, then sauté the onion over low heat until it is soft.

Add the crushed peppercorns, white wine and bayleaf.

Stir over high heat to release the alcohol and reduce the liquid by half.

Add the chicken stock and cream. Simmer and reduce by two-thirds (to approximately 300 ml).

Remove the bayleaf.

Serve with chicken or lamb.

BLACK PEPPER SAUCE *and* WHITE PEPPER SAUCE

HONEYED ROSELLA FLOWERS

200 GRAMS FROZEN ROSELLA FLOWERS
  (AVAILABLE FROM BUSH TUCKER
  SUPPLIERS OR GOOD DELICATESSENS)

150 GRAMS SUGAR

2 TABLESPOONS HONEY

¼ TEASPOON CORNFLOUR

1 TABLESPOON WATER

Heat the frozen rosella flowers and sugar in a pan until the sugar is dissolved. (Do not overcook or flowers will break up.) Add the honey. Dissolve the cornflour in water.

Remove the pan from the heat and quickly add the cornflour paste around the outer edge of the rosella mixture (this is the coolest part of the mixture). Stir constantly to avoid lumps.

Serve with lamb or game dishes.

SEAFOOD TOMATO SAUCE

2 TABLESPOONS OLIVE OIL

2 ONIONS, ROUGHLY CHOPPED

2 STICKS CELERY, SLICED

1 TABLESPOON GARLIC, CHOPPED

3–5 FRESH CHILLIES, CUT IN HALF AND
  SEEDED

1 CUP WHITE WINE

1 CUP WHITE WINE VINEGAR

1 CUP TOMATO PASTE

1 CUP SUGAR

2 BAY LEAVES

1 SPRIG FRESH THYME

3 WHOLE CLOVES

1 LITRE SEAFOOD STOCK (SEE PAGE 153)

Heat the oil, then sauté the onions, celery, garlic and chillies until they are soft.

Add all the other ingredients and simmer the mixture slowly until it reduces to 500 ml.

Place the sauce in a food processor or blender and blend until smooth.

Pass through a fine sieve.

HONEYED ROSELLA FLOWERS

CHUNKY TOMATO *and* RED WINE SAUCE

1 TABLESPOON OLIVE OIL

1 ONION, MEDIUM DICED

1 LITRE RED WINE

250 GRAMS WHITE SUGAR

1 TABLESPOON FRESH TARRAGON LEAVES

1 SPRIG THYME

4 LARGE, FIRM VINE-RIPENED TOMATOES,
    PEELED, SEEDED AND CUT INTO 2 CM DICE

1 TEASPOON CORNFLOUR

1 TABLESPOON WATER

SALT AND PEPPER TO TASTE

Heat the olive oil. Sauté the onion until soft.

Add the red wine, sugar, tarragon and thyme.

Simmer until the sauce reduces by three-quarters to 250 ml.

Remove the thyme stem.

Dissolve the cornflour in water.

Remove the pan from the heat and quickly add the cornflour paste around the outer edge of the sauce, stirring constantly.

Add the tomato pieces and gently warm them through for approximately 1 minute. Season. (Do not overcook or the tomato will loose its juices and thin the sauce.)

This is an extremely versatile sauce; serve it with fish, chicken, lamb or beef.

VARIATIONS

Add a few mushrooms, sautéed in butter.

Add 1 sliced capsicum, sautéed in oil.

Add small pitted black olives.

Substitute coriander for the tarragon and add a chopped chilli.

CHUNKY TOMATO *and* RED WINE SAUCE

TART BERRY JAM

200 GRAMS FRESH BLUEBERRIES

200 GRAMS WHITE SUGAR

1 TABLESPOON FRESH TARRAGON LEAVES, CHOPPED

3 TABLESPOONS BALSAMIC VINEGAR

1 TABLESPOON OLIVE OIL

Place the frozen berries and sugar in a heated pan and cook until the sugar has just dissolved.

Remove from the heat and add the tarragon, balsamic vinegar and oil.

Serve lukewarm.

Makes a delightful garnish for duck or lamb.

Especially good with game or turkey.

Note: Freezing the berries before cooking stops them from breaking up and helps to retain their shape.

RED BERRY JAM

100 GRAMS FROZEN LOGANBERRIES

100 GRAMS FROZEN BLACKBERRIES

200 GRAMS SUGAR

1 TABLESPOON FRESH TARRAGON LEAVES, CHOPPED

1 TABLESPOON BALSAMIC VINEGAR

1 TABLESPOON OLIVE OIL

Proceed as for Tart Berry Jam.

Note: Try substituting cranberries and redcurrants for the loganberries and blackberries – this makes a particularly good accompaniment for the Christmas turkey.

TART BERRY JAM *and* RED BERRY JAM

CHILLI JAM

2 TABLESPOONS OLIVE OIL

1 RED SPANISH ONION, DICED

1 LARGE RED CAPSICUM, SEEDED AND
ROUGHLY CHOPPED

1 PUNNET CHERRY TOMATOES

5 FRESH RED CHILLIES, SEEDED AND
CHOPPED

2 SPRIGS CORIANDER, STEMS AND LEAVES
CHOPPED FINELY

½ CUP BROWN SUGAR

4 TABLESPOONS CHILLI PASTE

2 TABLESPOONS FISH SAUCE

1 LEMON, PEELED, SEEDED AND CHOPPED

2 DROPS TABASCO SAUCE

SALT AND PEPPER TO TASTE

Heat the olive oil, then sauté the onion and capsicum until they are soft.

Add all the other ingredients and simmer slowly for 30 minutes, stirring occasionally.

Transfer the mixture to a food processor or blender and blend until smooth.

Adjust the seasoning.

Serve with fish or seafood.

Note: This recipe is quite hot, so feel free to adjust the amount of chilli paste.

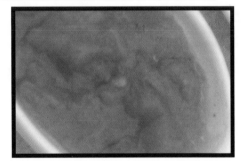 

CHILLI CHUTNEY *and* MANGO *and* CHILLI CHUTNEY

CHILLI CHUTNEY

100 GRAMS RED CHILLIES, SEEDED AND
   CHOPPED

1 TABLESPOON OLIVE OIL

500 GRAMS RED CAPSICUMS, ROASTED,
   SKINS REMOVED, SEEDED AND CHOPPED

1 WHITE ONION, FINELY CHOPPED

1 TEASPOON GARLIC, FINELY CHOPPED

100 GRAMS WHITE SUGAR

100 ML WHITE WINE VINEGAR

1 TEASPOON CINNAMON POWDER

Blend the chillies in a food processor or blender to make a paste. Put this aside.

Heat the olive oil, then sauté the capsicums, onion and garlic until they are soft.

Add the sugar, vinegar and cinnamon.

Add the chilli mixture.

Simmer on slow heat for approximately 20 minutes or until the mixture has thickened.

Serve with fish, seafood and white meats.

MANGO *and* CHILLI CHUTNEY

½ CUP WHITE WINE VINEGAR

½ CUP WHITE SUGAR

1 LARGE MANGO, PEELED AND CUT INTO
   THIN STRIPS

½ RED SPANISH ONION, CUT INTO
   SMALL DICE

1 TABLESPOON GREEN PEPPERCORNS

1 TABLESPOON FRESH TARRAGON LEAVES,
   CHOPPED

1 TABLESPOON FRESH FLAT-LEAF PARSLEY,
   CHOPPED

1 RED CHILLI, SEEDED AND CUT INTO
   VERY FINE DICE

2 DROPS TABASCO SAUCE

1 TABLESPOON OLIVE OIL

Warm the vinegar in a pan, then dissolve the sugar in it.

Remove the vinegar from the heat and add all the other ingredients.

Turn gently to combine.

Cover and leave for 2 hours to blend the flavours.

Serve at room temperature with fish or white meat salads.

MANGO AND MINT CHUTNEY VARIATION

Substitute 1 teaspoon of chopped fresh coriander leaves and 4 tablespoons of finely sliced fresh mint leaves for the tarragon and parsley.

WHITE ONION COMPOTE

500 GRAMS WHITE ONIONS, PEELED AND
  CUT INTO THIN JULIENNE SLICES

1 LITRE OF WATER

500 ML WHITE WINE

1 BAYLEAF

1 SPRIG THYME

2 TABLESPOONS WHITE SUGAR

SALT AND WHITE PEPPER TO TASTE

Poach the onions in water for approximately 20 minutes or until they are soft. (This removes any bitterness and keeps the compote white.) Strain.

Place the onions in a clean pan with the white wine, bayleaf, thyme and sugar.

Bring to the boil, then simmer, stirring constantly, until the mixture is thick and soft (approximately 40 minutes). Add the seasoning.

This makes an ideal accompaniment for salmon, game or venison. Serve warm or at room temperature.

VARIATION

For an Eastern flavour, add 2 tablespoons of minced ginger with the wine, herbs and sugar.

CHERRY TOMATO COMPOTE

3 TABLESPOONS OLIVE OIL

1 CLOVE GARLIC, FINELY CHOPPED

6 SPRING ONIONS, FINELY SLICED

1 TEASPOON WHITE SUGAR

500 GRAMS CHERRY TOMATOES, WASHED
  AND DRAINED

2 TABLESPOONS BASIL LEAVES, SLICED VERY
  FINELY

1 TEASPOON FLAT-LEAF PARSLEY, FINELY
  CHOPPED

SALT

CRUSHED BLACK PEPPER

Heat the oil, then sauté the garlic and spring onions until the garlic is soft (approximately 2 minutes).

Add the sugar and cherry tomatoes, then sauté the mixture for a further 4 minutes or until the skins are just starting to split. (The time will depend on the size of the cherry tomatoes.)

Remove from the heat and add the basil.

Serve hot or lukewarm as a garnish for lamb, chicken or fish.

VARIATIONS

Add 200 grams of sliced button mushrooms, sautéed in a little butter.

Add 1 red and 1 green capsicum, sliced and sautéed in 1 tablespoon of olive oil.

Substitute coriander leaves for the basil.

CAJUN PASTE

1 TABLESPOON CURRY POWDER

1 TABLESPOON CHILLI POWDER

2 TABLESPOONS SWEET PAPRIKA

1 TABLESPOON CRUSHED BLACK PEPPER

6 TABLESPOONS OLIVE OIL

1 TEASPOON SUGAR

SALT TO TASTE

Combine all the ingredients in a blender and mix to a paste.

Notes: Use as a marinade for beef, lamb or chicken. Spread a teaspoon on top of grilled fish, then grill for a further 2 minutes.

VARIATIONS

Fry 1 tablespoon of Cajun Paste for a few minutes to release the aromas, then add 300 ml of Watermark Demi-glaze (see page 170). Simmer to combine the flavours. Serve with beef or steak.

Add 1 tablespoon of Cajun Paste to 250 ml Ginger and White Wine Sauce (see page 157). Simmer to combine. Serve with fish for a spicy alternative.

Add 1–2 tablespoons of Cajun Paste to 500 ml fish, chicken or duck stock and use as the base for a Cajun soup.

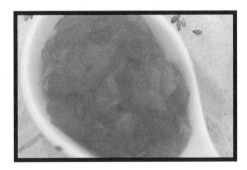 

WHITE ONION COMPOTE *and* CAJUN PASTE

WATERMARK DEMI-GLAZE

1 KG VEAL BONES, PREFERABLY VEAL SHANKS (HAVE YOUR BUTCHER CHOP THESE INTO PIECES)

1 CARROT, WASHED AND ROUGHLY CHOPPED

1 ONION, SKIN ON, WASHED AND ROUGHLY CHOPPED

1 CELERY STICK, WASHED AND ROUGHLY CHOPPED

1 CUP TOMATO PASTE

500 ML RED WINE

2 LITRES WATER

½ TEASPOON CRACKED BLACK PEPPERCORNS

1 BAYLEAF

1 SPRIG THYME

1 SPRIG ROSEMARY

Roast the veal bones, carrot, onion and celery in a hot oven at 200°C for 1½ hours or until thoroughly browned.

Add the tomato paste and mix it well with the bones and vegetables. Roast for a further 30 minutes.

Place the roasted bones and vegetables in a stockpot and deglaze the roasting pan with red wine, scraping all the brown bits from the bottom.

Add this liquid to the stockpot along with the water, peppercorns, bayleaf, thyme and rosemary.

Simmer, skimming occasionally, until the liquid reduces to 500 ml (approximately 2 hours).

Strain, allow to cool, then refrigerate.

Remove any fat from the surface.

VARIATIONS

For a lamb demi-glaze, substitute lamb bones.

For a game demi-glaze, substitute game bones.

For a beef demi-glaze, substitute beef marrow bones.

Notes: This is not thickened with flour. To create a strong, syrup-like sauce, simply reduce further.

This recipe can be doubled and frozen.

PRE-ROASTED DUCK

2 X NO. 12 DUCKS

1 TABLESPOON VEGETABLE OIL

1 TEASPOON SALT

1 TEASPOON SOY SAUCE

$\frac{1}{2}$ CUP VEGETABLE OIL

Wash the ducks well and rub the oil, salt and soy sauce into the skin.

Heat the oil in a roasting dish and roast the ducks, breast side up, in a very hot oven at 220°C for 30 minutes.

Baste with hot oil every 10 minutes.

Remove to a clean plate and allow to cool.

Note: This simple recipe is the first step in creating deliciously tender and fat-free duck dishes.

CORN MASH

80 GRAMS BUTTER

2 CUPS FRESH SWEET CORN KERNELS, BLANCHED

6 POTATOES, COOKED AND MASHED

$\frac{1}{4}$ TEASPOON NUTMEG

SALT AND PEPPER TO TASTE

Sauté the corn in 1 tablespoon of the butter for 2–3 minutes.

Add the mashed potato.

Stir in the remaining butter, nutmeg and seasoning.

Serve hot.

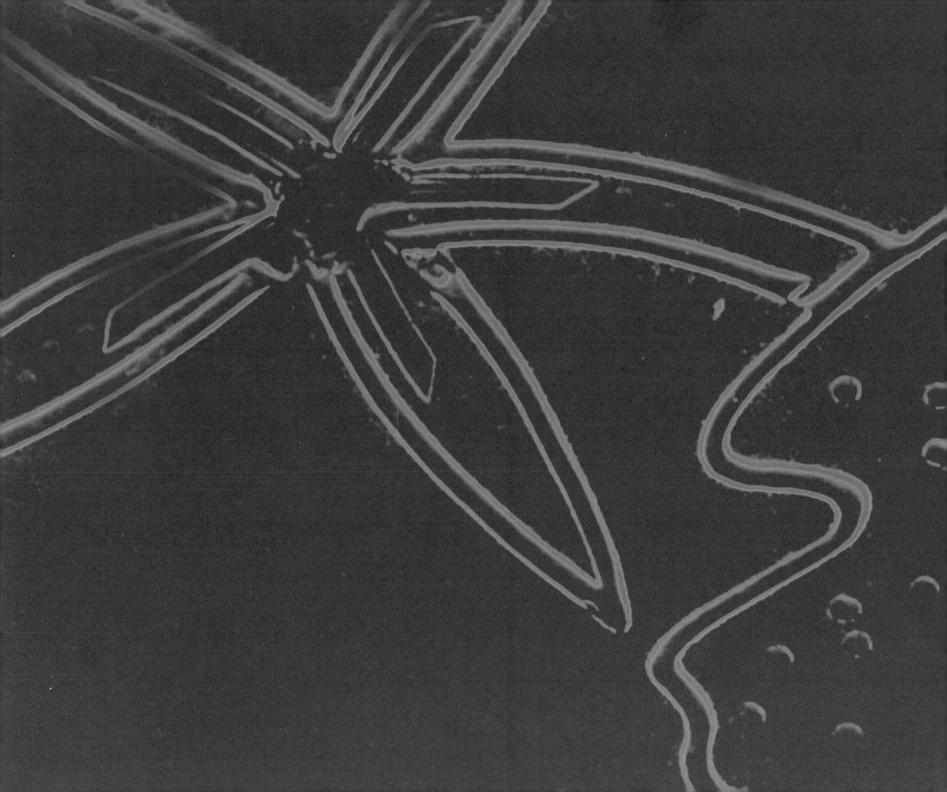